W9-BMB-885

Praise for Ariel and Shya Kane and *Working on Yourself Doesn't Work*

"I strongly recommend this book! Ariel and Shya Kane are highly skilled, experienced guides who point the way to the clarity of the present moment. They are at the forefront in the field of personal transformation and have much to offer anyone who wants a more meaningful and fulfilling life."
—Paul English, Publisher, *New York Spirit* magazine

"As a physicist I don't know how they do it. But my life has transformed by being around the Kanes. When serious life events have come up—prostrate cancer, my son disabled by a brain tumor, losing a job due to downsizing—I have been able to remain on-center and engaged in my life, not a victim."
—William R. Ellis, Ph.D., Vice President, Advanced Technology, Raytheon Company

"In an era of technological revolutions affecting how we work and how we communicate, the Kanes are creating a revolution in how we live."
—Andrew Gideon, Vice President, TAG Online, Inc.

"#1 Best Book Buy. 10+ Rating! A must for the library of every seeker of truth!"
—*Awareness* magazine

"Ariel and Shya Kane teach tools for living in the moment and undoing the knee-jerk behaviors that get in the way of living life with ease."

—*Time Out New York*

"Don't let the title mislead you. *Working on Yourself Doesn't Work* is not about the futility of self-improvement but rather about the effortlessness of transformation. . . . A simple, easy-to-read book with a valuable message that can take you through the swamp of the mind into the clarity and brilliance of the moment."

—*Whole Life Times* magazine

"This warm, accessible book will illuminate and befriend your transformation."

Personal Transformation magazine

"This book is a must read. One to have on your bookshelf and to share with your friends."

—*To Your Health* magazine

"Ariel and Shya Kane actually 'walk the talk.' . . . This simple yet profound book teaches us how to live in the moment. *Working on Yourself Doesn't Work* is refreshing, truthful, sincere, and authentic and written with insightfulness and clarity."

—Dr. Maryel McKinley

Working on Yourself Doesn't Work

The
3 Simple Ideas That Will Instantaneously Transform Your Life

ARIEL & SHYA KANE

New York Chicago San Francisco Lisbon London Madrid Mexico City
Milan New Delhi San Juan Seoul Singapore Sydney Toronto

Library of Congress Cataloging-in-Publication Data

Kane, Ariel.
    Working on yourself doesn't work : the 3 simple ideas that can instantaneously
transform your life / by Ariel & Shya Kane. — [Rev. ed.].
            p.   cm.
    ISBN-13: 978-0-07-160108-5 (alk. paper)
    ISBN-10: 0-07-160108-2 (alk. paper)
    1. Self-actualization (Psychology).   I. Kane, Shya.   II. Title.

    BF637.S4K33   2009
    158.1—dc22   2008009847

Excerpt from *Hsin-hsin Ming* by Seng-ts'an on page 130 reprinted with permission of
White Pine Press (whitepine.org)

4 5 6 7 8 9 DOC/DOC 1 9 8 7 6 5 4 3 2 1 0

ISBN 978-0-07-160108-5
MHID   0-07-160108-2

Illustrations by Barnett Plotkin
Interior design by designforbooks.com

McGraw-Hill books are available at special quantity discounts to use as premiums and
sales promotions or for use in corporate training programs. To contact a representative,
please visit the Contact Us pages at www.mhprofessional.com.

Instantaneous Transformation is a registered trademark.

This book is printed on acid-free paper.

When Shya was little, he asked his mother, Ida, why people were so unhappy and why there was so much pain and suffering in the world.

She replied, "I don't know. It has always been this way. When you grow up, maybe you can do something about it."

For our parents:

Geri and Don
Max and Ida

and for all those who ever dreamed of making a difference.

CONTENTS

PREFACE

Einstein said, "No problem can be solved from the same consciousness that created it. We must learn to see the world anew."

Yet how can you learn to see the world anew? What can you do to create a future that doesn't simply repeat the past or incrementally improve on what you had before? How can you have quantum leaps in the quality of your life?

After years of passionate inquiry into many different modalities of self-improvement, the two of us finally realized the startling answer to these questions: working on yourself doesn't work. Ultimately we discovered this moment and Instantaneous Transformation.

Having fallen ourselves into most of the pitfalls that keep a person from being in the moment, we are experienced guides who now bring people through the swamp of the mind into the clarity and brilliance of the moment.

In this book, we will introduce our Three Principles of Instantaneous Transformation and outline how these three simple ideas can act as an access point into the moment and a gateway to inner peace. We will not only highlight concepts that will unlock your true potential, but we will also outline the inhibitors to living your life directly. By living your life directly we mean that you will be empowered in your ability to experience life, take action, and be yourself rather than think about what to do next and worry whether or not you are doing your life right.

In the pages ahead, we will define and demonstrate what we mean by awareness, a nonjudgmental observation that completes previously unwanted habitual behaviors. By simply noticing how you are without judging yourself for what you see, you will strengthen your ability to be present and centered and experience well-being regardless of the circumstances.

Most of us have learned that we need to be hard on ourselves in order to change or get rid of unwanted conditions. Contrary to popular belief, if you do not judge yourself and if you are not hard on yourself for your "bad" habits, you will become neither stagnant nor complacent in your life. It has been our experience while working with thousands of people from all walks of life, from many different cultures all over the world, that when a person lives his or her life with awareness, that individual is self-empowered and becomes more productive, effective, and satisfied.

In the chapters ahead, we will also explore the difference between change and transformation so that you no longer have to create a future that repeats the past or is at best marginally better than what you had before.

We invite you to join us and discover the skill of truly living in the moment, day in, day out, not just when the circumstances of your life happen to be easy. The simple yet profound ideas contained in this book will support you in realizing the effortlessness of Instantaneous Transformation, spontaneously creating quantum leaps in the quality of your life.

ACKNOWLEDGMENTS

We thank all of the masters who came before, leaving a legacy of enlightenment, and all those with whom we have had the opportunity to study on our own paths to self-discovery.

Like our lives, Instantaneous Transformation is a living, breathing, and evolving entity. On any given day, the community of people who are actively participating or who are peripherally involved is evolving and changing as well. We thank all those whose paths have intersected with ours in our seminars and consulting sessions. By sharing your lives and your life circumstances you have empowered us to discover and define the technology of Instantaneous Transformation. Many of you will recognize yourselves in the examples used throughout *Working on Yourself Doesn't Work*.

Thanks also to the folks over at White Pine Press, especially publisher Dennis Maloney, for graciously letting us use an excerpt from their lovely little book *Hsin-hsin Ming*, by Seng-ts'an.

Thanks to our brother-in-law, Barnett (Barney) Plotkin, whose illustrations have added a whole new dimension to our work—you live on in this book.

Last but not least, we are very thankful to all those who have encouraged us over the years and have faithfully told us the truth, without whom we are certain *Working on Yourself Doesn't Work* would still be a dream and not a reality.

INTRODUCTION

Countless numbers of us have done therapy of one sort or another. Those seeking well-being have taken seminars on subjects ranging from our wounded inner child to time management, investing time and money in everything from meditation retreats to walking on fire and high-energy effectiveness trainings. Most of us have analyzed our lives, planned our days, changed our diets, visualized our goals, and prayed for guidance.

And yet, for the two of us, after attending hundreds of seminars and courses and reading plenty of inspirational books, there was still a sense of emptiness. After each seminar, retreat, or book, we would have a new system through which to view life. We would feel hyped up or enthusiastic about ourselves, sometimes even changed and revitalized, but sooner or later we would be lying awake at night thinking, "There has got to be more to life than this."

At first we could blame the emptiness on goals. We hadn't met our goals. So we took yet another course where we wrote lists, made plans, visualized, and strategized, employing the Laws of Attraction to produce the things we wanted, things we thought were missing that should finally produce that sense of well-being that was so illusive.

Life became very difficult for the two of us when this visualization approach "worked." Soon after we got the things we had been targeting—the co-op apartment on Park Avenue in Manhattan, the successful careers, not to mention loads of friends and a great relationship—the emptiness, that feeling that we were missing something, got too strong to be ignored.

There was a quiet desperation within each of us to do our lives "right," to "make a difference," and yet even volunteering our time to help others only created momentary blips of "OK-ness" within ourselves while privately in our heart of hearts we were unhappy, bereft of true well-being.

Our lives at this time were a pendulum swinging between identifying a problem and coming up with a reasonable solution. At this point, we figured that acquiring things and living for the future must be the source of our dissatisfaction. Following this logic, we thought that if we simplified, divested ourselves of everything, and learned how to meditate, we would produce that fleeting state of happiness.

So we quit. We sold the Park Avenue apartment, and we had a New York City version of a garage sale and sold all our things. We bought two backpacks and some supplies and set off to see the world. Actually, we only got as far as northern Italy. The beginning of our world tour included a stop at a meditation center where we had booked yet another three-week workshop. However, this time, something was different. When we got to this center, we stopped running from the emptiness—running from ourselves.

We stayed there for the better part of two years, examining and questioning everything: our thoughts, our culture, our truth, and even whether we should continue being together. We participated in groups, many a month long, on healing, breath, movement, intuition, massage, and an advanced counselor's training. The last workshop we did was a six-month-long, twenty-four-hour-a-day meditation intensive.

At the end of these six months, it was the end of thinking that meditation was the answer. By now we had managed to spend almost all of the money we had gotten from selling the apartment. Our credit cards were maxed out, but at least we still had each other.

It was time to reenter the real world, so we returned to the United States, borrowed a car from Ariel's parents, drove to San Francisco, and rented a room. A few months after arriving in California we attended an evening given by the people who had headed the meditation center in Italy. It was actually here that we realized that their dedication was to "work on" issues and they encouraged others to follow this approach. Seeing this, we suddenly, spontaneously realized that Working on Yourself Doesn't Work and that, in fact, working on yourself produces an endless cycle of pain.

It became apparent to us that these well-meaning folks were running down empty paths, cul-de-sacs filled with pain and suffering. We saw that their path and ours were going in different directions and we had to find our own.

It was around this time we started discovering that we were rich. Although we had very little in the way of money, we felt well in ourselves. We were in love. We felt fulfilled, and even though we were not sure what we would do next in our lives, we were not worried; we were at peace. At night we were reading aloud to each other from a book called *The Unborn: The Life and Teachings of Zen Master Bankei,* which is a book of a seventeenth-century Zen master's dissertations and teachings on the subject of Self-Realization. One day, while walking up the hill from the beach, Shya realized that he was living in a manner consistent with the Self-Realized state described in that book. At that moment, he declared himself "done" working on himself. It was a gutsy move. By extension he instantaneously stopped working on Ariel, too. Within a day or two, the impact of this new reality began to truly manifest itself. We discovered unplumbed depths of compassion for ourselves and each other. We truly had spontaneously stopped working on ourselves and each other.

This Instantaneous Transformation became apparent to our friends as well. People wanted to know what had happened. "You are so different," they said. Just being around us made them feel centered and at peace with themselves. They invited us to speak with them and their friends . . . and our first workshops were born.

We were now embarking on a grand new adventure— the adventure of a lifetime. We had to define and communicate this new essence of how we lived and approached life. This was a challenge. How does one express what is inexpressible in words? Once we had begun living life with a moment-to-moment sense of well-being, we had forgotten that our state of being wasn't the norm. When we let go of the past, we quickly forgot all of the pain and striving that had been so much a part of our daily existence. Having gone through as much as we had in our lives, independently and together, we discovered we had a knack for being incredibly insightful. Now, when we see people in pain, vainly running down the fruitless roads that we have traveled, we can say, "We know you. We have been there. It doesn't have to take as long for you as it did for us. You can get here today, now, this instant." And it's true. Through our Instantaneous Transformation technology, people are finding their true selves quickly. It's exciting. We have seen over and over, regardless of age, race, sex, nationality, or religion, people's lives transform—instantaneously. You don't need to work on yourself. Just getting into this moment is enough.

This book can facilitate personal, individual transformation. By presenting a blend of our ideas and personal experiences we have addressed many of the recurring themes we have seen in our workshops.

Please don't take this book too seriously. And please don't believe what we say. Lord knows none of us needs another belief system. If you like, you can pretend you are reading a fantasy novel, a mystery, or perhaps good science fiction.

And maybe, just maybe, you will bump into yourself along the way.

1

HOW TO USE THIS BOOK

*T*he choices we face today are certainly more baffling than they were a hundred years ago, when societal roles were preset and people could blindly follow the cultural prescription. Increasingly, individuals have the power to make their own way. No longer are we living in small communities with few options outside of the standards, mores, and ideals of those around us. With the advent of air travel, we can move great distances in a short period of time. Through television, other cultures and global events appear in our living rooms. Using the Internet, a vast array of information is just a click away, providing us with options and alternatives we would never have come up with on our own. No longer is gender the determining factor when choosing an occupation. As we each travel down our own unique path, questions arise: Is what I am doing right? Am I with the right person? Is this the job for me? Do I want children? Should I move? How can I be sure?

With the myriad of possibilities facing us today, we want to feel confident that our choices are good ones. We want to be strong in ourselves but not rigid. We want to feel that our lives have direction, purpose, and meaning.

Heaven on Earth is happening simultaneously with the way our lives are showing up, right now in this moment. The trick is to be able to access this coexisting state, day in, day out, moment by moment, not just when in pleasant, ideal circumstances.

We read, search, and exchange ideas in hopes of being centered, being productive, and feeling vital. We are looking for something to transform a mundane existence into an exciting, breathtaking adventure, searching for peace of mind, health, and satisfaction. What people pine for in their secret hearts has been described by sages throughout the ages as Enlightenment and Self-Realization. There are other synonyms too—nirvana, waking up, the Great Way, heaven on earth, Christ Consciousness, or realizing your Higher Self.

The two of us have spent the better part of our adult lives in search of the miraculous. We hungered for that state of being wherein satisfaction, self-expression, and creativity reside. We took countless workshops and traveled to be with masters all over the world in search of this elusive state, only to discover that Enlightenment, Self-Realization, and Self-Satisfaction coexist with our present state of being.

In the following pages, we will define the keys that open the door to living in the moment that will facilitate a transformational shift, enabling you to live a more effective, productive, and satisfying life. We will also outline impediments to living in a vitally, alive manner. But first let us present a few concepts that will support you in getting the most out of this book.

PARADOX AND CONFUSION

It has been said that the doors to enlightenment are guarded by two lions. One of the lions represents paradox. As you read on, you may find some ideas seem paradoxical—in other words, it may seem that we are presenting two ideas that are directly in opposition to each other. A paradox is where these two seemingly contradictory ideas can both be true. For example, take the saying "water, water everywhere and not a drop to drink." One might think if there is water everywhere, of course you could drink it. Yet if you were floating in the middle of the ocean on a raft, this statement would not only be true but also make perfect sense. As you continue reading *Working on Yourself Doesn't Work*, if you come across ideas that seem to contradict each other, we suggest you hold your disagreement in abeyance and relax around them. As you let the ideas settle in, you may discover an expanded way of seeing that resolves the apparent opposition.

The other lion represents confusion. It is likely that you will find some of the concepts in this book confusing at first. This is a natural process because anything that is new, that is outside your current reality, will not make immediate sense.

There are two main reasons for confusion. The first is when something doesn't fit what is already known, the mind gets confused trying to find a place for it, trying to make it fit, trying to make sense out of it. The second reason is to avoid the domination of the information being presented. In other words, people get confused when information goes against an agenda they are currently holding. For example, the suggestion that you can let go of your past and it no longer has to determine how you live your life today, in this moment, can feel extremely confusing to someone who is determined to prove that his or her parents have caused irreparable damage by their child-rearing techniques. If you are committed to proving a point of view, such as "My parents screwed me up," then confusion is an effective device to avoid giving up that point of view.

In Zen, there is a term *beginner's mind*. In the beginner's mind there is no preconception of already knowing or having heard something before. There is only the possibility of something new, something heretofore unseen. When reading this, if you could view the information as fresh, and actually hear what we're saying, your whole life could transform in an instant.

LISTENING YOUR WAY TO THE MOMENT

One way to access the moment is to truly hear what others are saying. If you listen newly to each individual conversation, the act of listening can shift your life instantaneously. It does this by pulling you into the moment. And the moment is magic. Transformation happens when one gets into the current moment of now. Here is an example:

A man named Cecil was walking down Second Avenue in Manhattan one Monday evening and noticed our poster announcing an Instantaneous Transformation evening seminar. Intrigued, he came in and joined us. A rather private man, Cecil sat quietly toward the back of the room. Over the course of the evening different people stood and spoke about what was happening in their lives. One of these was a man in his early sixties, Glenn, who asked a question about the Second Principle of Instantaneous Transformation. We will present the Three Principles of Instantaneous Transformation in depth in the chapters ahead, but let us just say here that we were discussing how you can only physically be where you are in any given moment.

During this conversation we talked about how no two things can occupy the same space at the same time; in other words, no two people could be seated in the exact same chair at the exact same moment. In fact, from moment to moment, you can only be where you are and how you are. This includes your body sensations, emotions, thoughts, feelings, and life circumstances. (Again, this is the Second Principle of Instantaneous Transformation.) As the discussion continued, we talked with Glenn about how he could only be standing and having this conversation with us in that moment. He might have the thought he could be in Hawaii, for instance, but in reality he was in New York City. Cecil heard the discussion and had a direct experience of the truth of it.

One week later, Cecil returned. And here is what he had to say: "Hello, Ariel and Shya. Hello, everyone, my name is Cecil and I didn't speak last week but I listened and something remarkable has happened. I feel so free—free in a way that I never felt before. Let me explain: I come from South Africa, and two years ago my mother fell ill and she died and I was unable to be with her. I have had such tremendous guilt, such heaviness and pain. Every day I was so hard on myself that I wasn't there to hold her hand at the time of her passing. I had been berating myself for two years. Suddenly, I heard something you said to Glenn. I simply realized that I could not have been there when my mother died for no other reason than the fact that I wasn't. It wasn't good; it wasn't bad. It just was the truth. I don't know why or how this happened, but the heavy burden spontaneously lifted. I am no longer plagued by guilt. It happened in an instant. I don't understand it, but I guess I don't have to. I am very, very grateful."

If you truly listen to what somebody is saying, not by comparing what he or she is saying to what you already know or agreeing or disagreeing with what is being said, but if you are listening to hear it from the other point of view, this act of listening is enough to pull you into the moment. However, you have an incredibly facile mind. You can race ahead in your thoughts and finish another person's sentence before he or she gets to the point. Or you can take exception to a word he or she uses and stop listening altogether. If you pay attention, you will see that there are many times when you have an internal commentary on what is being said rather than just listening. If you can train yourself to hear what is being said, from the speaker's point of view, it takes you outside of time and into the current moment. This is a magical space where, once accessed, the by-product is Instantaneous Transformation.

The act of listening pulls you into the moment, and the moment is where transformation happens. Transformation is not something that happens in the future; it only happens in the present moment of now. Being fully engaged in an activity pulls you into the moment, which sets the stage for transformation. In the case of this book, we suggest reading without adding anything, such as applying it to your life while reading, agreeing or disagreeing with what is being said, or commenting to yourself as you go. The act of reading will then be akin to truly listening, and it will access the moment, thus creating the possibility of Instantaneous Transformation.

> True Listening is actively listening to another with the intention of hearing what is being said from the other's point of view.

COMPARISON

When it is grappling with something new or unfamiliar, the mind finds something it already knows, which it perceives as a reasonable facsimile, and then groups the two together. In essence, the mind compares what is new in this moment to its memory bank of moments to help it understand something, to give it a context. This is almost always off target. Comparison limits the possibility of living in the moment. At best, it cuts out the nuances of living, and it is in the nuances where the richness of life is born. At worst, our interpretations are totally inaccurate.

When a friend of ours was little, she heard the song "My Bonnie Lies over the Ocean." She had never heard of a "bonnie." It wasn't in her vocabulary. So, instead, she interpreted what she heard as "My *body* lies over the ocean. My *body* lies over the sea . . ." Hearing the words she thought were part of the song would always bring to her mind images of someone floating on his or her back in the calm blue ocean. Now, as an adult, she realizes that she misinterpreted the lyrics. What seemed similar or the same was not the same at all. Whether we are old or young, our minds still function like that.

Here is another example of how it works. A number of years ago we were in Quepos, Costa Rica, when Marcella told us about her new business. She works at a charter sport fishing company where we had been clients for years. Marcella is a lovely woman with wavy hair and a boisterous nature. We liked to come into her office from time to time and sit in the cool of the air-conditioning and hear tales of what the fleet of sport fishing boats had caught and released in the previous days.

On one such day, she said to us, "You must come to visit me one evening at my new business! My boyfriend and I have opened a new topless bar. It is up the hill in Manuel Antonio."

She looked so proud. We were surprised.

"Do your bosses here know that you run a topless bar?"

"Oh, yes!" she exclaimed. "Maria and Patricio are two of our best customers."

We looked at each other. How could this be? We knew the owners of the fishing company were Italian, and perhaps they were more liberal than we knew. She made a topless bar sound so normal, sort of like going to McDonald's or Applebee's.

Trying not to let our eyes dip to her chest as we imagined the scene, one of us tactfully asked, "Do you work at the bar?"

"Oh, yes, I do. Mainly weekends but often on weeknights also. We're getting very busy. You can see our restaurant on the right, just after you pass the Barba Roja restaurant. Look for it and come in. I'll give you a free drink. We have all sorts of typical Costa Rican finger foods. You'll like it. You can bring your groups too."

We had a hard time imagining bringing the participants from one of our Self-Discovery Adventures to a topless bar, but we did our best to be gracious.

We left the fishing office that day amazed that there was a topless bar near the tiny fishing village. We had been going there for years, and, although there were many drinking establishments, sports bars, and eateries, we had never heard of or seen such a thing.

As our taxi took us up the hill to our hotel we scanned the roadside for any sign of Marcella's new topless bar, but we didn't see a thing. Several trips up and down that road didn't reveal its whereabouts even though she claimed it was easy to find.

The next week we went into the fishing office for the recent news and sat once again in front of Marcella. The conversation took an unexpected turn.

"I looked for you last week at my restaurant," she said.

"Yes, we looked for the sign but didn't see it."

"I was hoping you would come in for some tapas."

"Tapas? What are tapas?"

Marcella looked confused. "Tapas," she said. "You know, tapas bar or finger food bar. Food you eat with your fingers. That's what we serve. *Tapas* is the Costa Rican word for finger food. Obviously that's why we call it a tapas bar."

We burst out laughing and explained the joke. She had been saying *tapas*, which we heard as *topless* since we hadn't heard this word before. Our mental computers just filled in with what they knew as a reasonable facsimile. When we asked her about her *topless* bar, that word was so outside of her reality, she filled in with what she expected to hear, *tapas*.

As we left that day, we thought it was a good joke and an excellent example of how we only know what we know and how anything that is outside of our reality doesn't even exist. It also showed us how three people who were sincerely trying to communicate with each other could so totally and utterly misinterpret what was said.

2

WHERE ARE YOU?

*L*et's say you don't know where you are in New York City and you want to get to 72nd Street and Broadway. You can look at a road map and you can find out where Broadway and 72nd cross, but that alone won't help you. First you have to know where you are. If you don't know where you are in this moment, you'll never find where you want to be.

The starting point is to discover where you are. And then, when you know where you are in this moment, something can shift. This takes a degree of surrender to how the circumstances in your life are showing up.

When you are in water, if you relax, it floats you. If you struggle, if you tense up, you sink and drown. Well, it's that way with life.

If you are present with what's happening in your life in each moment, life supports you totally. But if you are worrying about possible futures, you're not present. It's as if you're breathing in when you're underwater. You sink and drown. That's why many people's lives feel overwhelming to them. It is a function of trying to live their life right rather than noticing who they're with, what they're doing, where they are in their life in this moment.

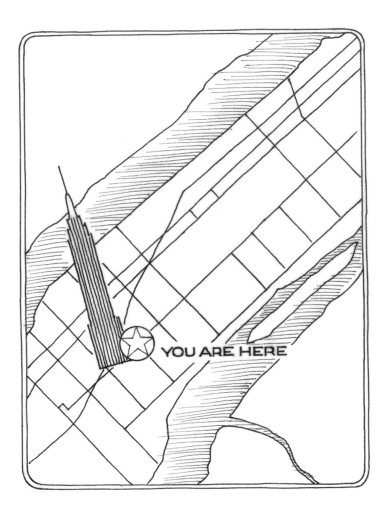

Noticing or neutrally observing your life without trying to manipulate or change what you see is actually the essence or key component of Instantaneous Transformation. Another word for this nonjudgmental seeing is *awareness*.

AWARENESS

You don't need to work on yourself. In order to be fulfilled, feel deeply satisfied, and live life to its fullest it is essential that you learn just to notice, to be aware.

What it takes to wake up or transform is to bring awareness to whatever is going on in your life in the moment. "Bringing awareness" does not mean you have to do something with what you become aware of. You don't have to do anything about it. You don't have to fix it or change it. You simply have to be aware.

As simple as it is, this is a hard concept for people to understand, because usually when people see something about themselves that they perceive as negative, they judge it and don't like it and try to change it. This is not awareness. Awareness is neutral.

Awareness is a non-judgmental seeing. It is an objective, noncritical seeing or witnessing of the nature or "isness" of any particular circumstance or situation. It is an ongoing process in which you are bringing yourself back to the moment, rather than complaining silently about what you perceive as wrong or what you would prefer.

When you become aware of a mechanical behavior such as biting your nails and just notice it, the automaticity actually fades away, and then you are left with you, acting appropriately, choosing whether or not to continue that behavior.

In the pages that follow you will find many examples of how simple awareness dissolves even profound pain, both emotional and physical.

THE PHENOMENON OF INSTANTANEOUS TRANSFORMATION

Transformation doesn't actually happen through words. Transformation is an experience, not a concept. But the mind can only hold concepts. For example, the difference between actually being on a warm sunny beach and thinking about being on a warm sunny beach is profound.

In addition, experiences naturally devolve into concepts. For example, let's say you develop a toothache one evening—it is throbbing and painful, and your jaw is swollen. It hurts so much that you cannot sleep, and you can hardly wait until morning when the dentist will be available. By the next morning, when the dentist can fit you in, even the vibration from walking jars your sensitive tooth. This experience, in the moment that you are having it, is very intense, and words cannot describe the depth of feeling. A week later, however, when trying to describe it to a friend, the description bears no resemblance to the actual physical sensations that you endured. The experience of the pain has now devolved into a concept, and your conversation about the experience falls way short of the real thing.

With transformation, in order to maintain something other than a temporary shift, there has to be a letting go of the habitual ways of thinking. Otherwise, the mind catches up with any transformation, compensates for it, and you are back where you started. That is why people have peak experiences, and they're just that—a peak that doesn't last. They get out of their mechanical way of relating for a bit, but then the mind gets back in control and they go right back into the old systems of behavior. Everything is again the same as it ever was.

There was a fellow who once came to an Instantaneous Transformation seminar we presented. From his perspective, the evening had a magical quality. He suddenly felt less worried. At work in the week afterward, he got things done with little or no effort. He slept well for the first time in years. He felt in sync with his whole life.

A year later, he came to another evening seminar very angry at us. "It was supposed to be instantaneous," he said, "but it only lasted for a few weeks."

This man was looking for a magic pill. He wanted to swallow it once and then not have to pay attention to how he was living for the rest of his life. What engendered the shift in the first place was that our seminar created an environment where this fellow could look at himself without finding fault with what he saw. The seminar acted as a neutral light, illuminating what simply was in his life so that he could see it without judgment.

The awareness that was brought forth in this group produced an instantaneous shift. But awareness is not a onetime thing. Bringing awareness to how you relate to yourself and your environment is a way of life. If you want transformational shifts to last, you must support them. You wouldn't expect to go to the gym and say, "Wow, what a great workout. Well, that should take care of exercise for the next five or ten years. See ya next decade." The ability to live moment to moment is like an underused skill or muscle. With practice it becomes strong and you are able to have stamina and endurance.

This is paradoxical. On the one hand, working on yourself doesn't work. On the other hand, you must be engaged in your life and aware of how you are living in order to have transformation be a lasting and expanding experience.

CHANGE VERSUS TRANSFORMATION

In the past, *transformation* was an obscure word, but this term has really made it into the mainstream in the last few years. It has gotten so that people think change and transformation are pretty much the same. But they are not.

We, as authors, are not trying to get you to manipulate your language so you say the right words after reading this book. Rather, we feel it is important that you know what we are talking about when using the term *transformation* as opposed to *change*. This next section is devoted to delineating the differences between the two so that you will be able to recognize and support the state of transformation.

Transformation can only be instantaneous. Anything that happens over time is change. Change is an incremental, linear progression. It happens over time. It is directed. It is measurable. It is provable. It is logical. It happens sequentially. Change follows the laws of cause and effect.

Transformation, on the other hand, is exponential, not incremental. It happens everywhere at once. It is not linear. It happens outside of time. It is instantaneous. It is an immediate exponential shift, like a shifting of states, and it goes forward and backward in time. It is a shift, like a molecule of water that goes from liquid to solid at the instant it hits thirty-two degrees Fahrenheit.

Change is past/future oriented, whereas transformation is now. Transformation is only now and it can only happen now, in the present moment. You cannot work on yourself to transform. Change involves *doing*, whereas transformation is a way of *being*.

For example, we know a woman who started dating again after feeling lonely for years. She thought she had to *do* something to make herself attractive rather than *be* herself, which already was attractive. The extra effort she made when she spoke with available men had the effect of diminishing her allure and pushing them away. When you are being yourself, being in the moment, it is not a behavior derived from your thoughts. In other words, you don't think how to be and then *do* that; it is a natural expression of yourself.

Again, transformation is a by-product of being in the moment, which happens through awareness, an objective, nonpreferential seeing or witnessing of the way you relate to your life circumstances, your feelings, your emotions,

When you get here—to this moment of now—each day becomes extraordinary. It is profound and ordinary at the same time.

and your thought processes. If you do not make yourself right or wrong for what you discover, those behaviors or ways of being will transform and lose their power over your life. When those mechanical behaviors cease to dominate you, you will discover who you really are—a being who happens to occupy your body, along with the mind, which dominates your life. When you are simply being, the mind loses its control over you. It then becomes a valuable tool rather than a mechanism that keeps you repeating old, limiting, nonsatisfying patterns of behavior.

Coming to know who you are is far simpler than most of us make it. Most of us have learned that we need to be hard on ourselves in order to change. What the two of us have discovered is that working on yourself doesn't work. We have discovered the effortlessness of transformation, which happens in an instant when you discover how to live in the moment.

Being in the moment allows you to include the conflicts that arise in your day, the body sensations, emotions, and so on. For instance, there are days when you do not feel well, but when you are living your life moment by moment, you can include uncomfortable feelings and sensations and still experience well-being.

A lot of people have the erroneous idea that when you transform you are never ill, never tired at the end of a day, and never have any human frailties. They think you should never get angry or be upset. This is not the case. When you really discover how to get here, you can integrate anything that happens in your life, so you experience a state of well-being out of which you live.

> Awareness is a non-judgmental witnessing, viewing, or seeing of yourself and how you interact with your life.

Again, what allows you to transform is awareness.

The Instantaneous Transformation technology is based in awareness. While change is psychological in nature and problem/solution oriented, transformation is anthropological. The job of anthropologists is to simply notate what they see in a culture or a tribe without judgmental interpretation. For example, they might say, "The tribe ate roasted grubs this morning at 6 A.M." This is a simple observation. A good anthropologist wouldn't say, "First thing these people did today was eat those disgusting grubs."

What we are suggesting is that there is an "isness" to things that is not culturally determined. Through awareness, you can notice what is, not what you consider beautiful or ugly, appealing or disgusting. Simply what is.

To dissolve unwanted behaviors, you need to interact with your own life as though you are an anthropologist studying a culture of one, yourself. An anthropologist suspends judgment, looks at the culture not as right or wrong or good or bad, simply observes how it operates and functions.

Within our own lives, most of us do not simply observe how we function. Rather, we judge ourselves, comparing how we are to how we think we ought to be based on cultural standards (or resistance to those standards).

We are all addicted to fixing what we perceive as our weaknesses and faults rather than observing ourselves neutrally. Transformation is not about fixing yourself to be a better you. It is about being the way you are.

If you simply see how you are without judging, manipulating, or trying to fix what you see, this will facilitate the completion of unwanted behaviors. In other words, if you don't energize your habits, they will naturally dwindle and dissolve all on their own. How? Neutrally observing something doesn't add energy to it—for or against—and everything in this universe needs energy to survive.

Change	Transformation
Happens over Time	Instantaneous
Past/Future	Present Moment
Linear/Incremental	Exponential/Quantum
Psychological	Anthropological
Cause/Effect	Observation/Awareness
Judgmental	Nonjudgmental
Dichotomous	Based in What Is/Isness
Good/Bad	
Right/Wrong	
Positive/Negative	
Win/Lose	
Mind/Survival Based	Aliveness Based
Reasonable/Logical	Unreasonable/Intuitive
Left Brain	Right Brain

Goal/Doing Oriented	Being Oriented
Problem/Solution	"Isness"
Decisions	Choices
Manipulative	Creative
Reactive	Proactive
Exclusive	Inclusive
Hierarchical	Partnership/Team

3

THE PRINCIPLES OF
INSTANTANEOUS
TRANSFORMATION

*W*hile reading this section, it is likely that you will come upon some radically new ideas. There is a phenomenon that takes place when one is confronted with learning any new skill: there are moments of clarity and understanding followed by a complete loss of clarity. You could call it "getting it" and then "losing it." This is normal when one grapples with something new. We suggest that you relax as you read about the Three Principles of Instantaneous Transformation and don't put pressure on yourself to fully understand them if you find some of the ideas confusing at first. It is unnecessary that you understand or remember it all. As this book progresses, we will give you several practical examples of the Three Principles that will bring the concepts into sharp focus so that you can use them in your own life. Then, if you wish, you can reread this section. It is likely that all of the pieces will have fallen into place all on their own.

Following are the Three Principles of Instantaneous Transformation.

The First Principle is this: **Anything you resist persists—and grows stronger.**

Chances are, those things that you want to change or fix about yourself have persisted, no matter how many times you have resolved to change them.

You become attached to anything you push against. If you resist something, at best you narrowly define yourself against the thing you are resisting; at worst you become just like the very thing you resist. Here is an example. Let's say that the fist in the illustration on the facing page represents your father, who you are resisting, and the open hand represents you. You push against your father because you resist him, and pretty soon the open hand has assumed the shape of your father and you become just like him in the opposite. "Rebels" are not truly free. Because they define themselves in opposition to their parents or their upbringing, they are actually controlled by what they resist. So anything you resist persists and sticks around.

If you want a more scientific explanation of this principle, it goes something like this: For every action there is an equal and opposite reaction.

The Second Principle is also a rule of physics: **No two things can occupy the same space at the same time.**

For example, if a person is sitting in a chair, no other person can sit in that exact spot in that same chair at the exact same time.

In the case of emotions, you cannot be happy if you are actually sad—no two emotions can occupy the exact same space at the exact same time.

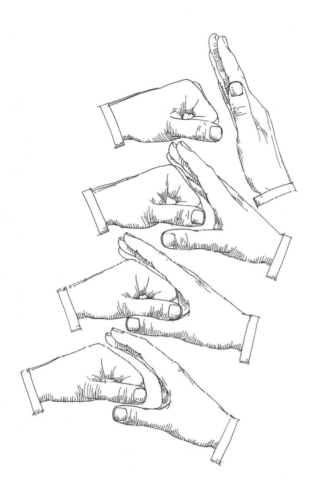

If you are seated while you are reading this page, you will discover that you can only be seated in this moment of now.

We all have been taught that we can improve our lot in life. But in this very moment of now, you can only be exactly as you are. Striving to attain an idea or an ideal is akin to saying the way you are is imperfect or flawed. You may have the idea that you can be different, but in reality, in this moment, you are the way you are.

If we were to take a photograph of you, at the moment the picture was taken you could only have been the way the camera captured you in that moment. You can't change the way you were. Life shows up in a series of moments of now, and in this moment of now you can only be exactly the way you are—and that is the Second Principle.

The Third Principle is as follows: **Anything that you allow to be exactly as it is will complete itself and disappear.**

In other words, if you let things actually be the way they are, without trying to change them or fix them, without judging them as good or bad or right or wrong, they complete themselves and disappear.

This includes psychological, physiological, and emotional pain as well as upsets. If you let yourself be upset when you are upset rather than trying to get rid of the feeling (First Principle: what you resist persists), then it will dissolve all on its own and disappear.

Have you noticed that happiness is fleeting? Do you resist it when it happens? Do you say, "Oh, no, I'm happy again. I was hoping this happiness wouldn't overtake me"? Happiness is not one of those things we usually resist. So it goes really quickly. But if we're upset or sad, these states have a tendency to linger because we generally don't want to be upset when we are upset or sad when we are sad. Disagreeing with how your life is showing up in this moment is a form of resistance. And don't forget, resistance results in the unwanted condition's persistence.

Look at your life—hasn't everything that you've tried to get rid of stuck around on some level? Those things that you push against, when you've said, "I've got to change. I shouldn't be like that," don't resolve. That's the First Principle.

Again, the Second Principle is "No two things can occupy the same space at the same time." In other words, if you allow yourself to feel what you're feeling when you're feeling it (that's the Third Principle), it will clear up; it will disappear.

Awareness, a nonjudgmental investigation, can free you from old patterns—even things that have gone on for years, that you've resisted, that you've tried to get rid of and have had New Year's resolutions about. If you allow yourself to simply be with anything, it loses its power over you. However, if you resist an old pattern of behavior, you give it power over your life

We are suggesting a way of being that involves surrendering to your life, not resisting the way your life shows up in each moment. Your life presents itself the way it does. It doesn't show up any differently. Again, you can't be standing when you are sitting. Now what you do with the way your life is showing up is up to you.

Let's come back to the First Principle. If you resist circumstances in your life, they persist. If on the other hand you simply notice your circumstances, without judging what you see, if you just say, "Oh, this is the way my life is, OK," then unwanted patterns complete themselves. However, you cannot "accept" something as a means to get rid of it, change it, or fix it. This is not acceptance at all. In actuality, acceptance with an agenda to change the situation is a manipulation to get to what you want rather than experiencing or being with what you have. Transformation doesn't work that way. But if you actually, genuinely choose to have what you have when you have it, it disappears.

When you allow yourself to be the way you are, and notice how you are being without judging yourself, a phenomenon takes place called completion. In other words, if you notice the way you behave without trying to change or fix yourself and without judging what you discover, those behaviors that you have been trying to change or ways of being that you have been putting up with will complete themselves, just with awareness. But you can't notice it to get rid of it, because that throws you back into the First Principle—anything you resist persists and grows stronger.

You can think of awareness like taking a block of ice and letting it sit in the sun. The radiant heat of simple awareness is enough to melt old, frozen mechanical behaviors.

OK, so now you have the Principles of Instantaneous Transformation in a conceptual form. Perhaps you would like a practical example.

OLD BLUE

In 1982, when the two of us were on our third date, there was a dramatic incident in which we had a firsthand experience that demonstrated the Principles of Instantaneous

Transformation in action. The following story is told from Ariel's point of view.

It was a beautiful Sunday morning in late August, and New York City seemed to be resting up for the week ahead. It was the kind of morning when you could see all the way up and down the avenues. What a glorious day for a ride to Jones Beach on the back of Shya's blue motorcycle, a Yamaha 650 Special, "Old Blue." We had bundled our towels and sunscreen behind the seat and, thus prepared, headed out of town.

It felt like flying. We both were dressed in shorts and T-shirts, our heads protected by helmets and visors, and the morning sun felt good on my skin. What an excellent day to be alive! Even the traffic lights seemed to be going our way.

Shortly after we breezed through the tunnel into Queens, we took an exit and made our way to an open gas station. Pulling up to the pump, Shya stood Old Blue on the kickstand and opened the tank to fill it up.

Deciding to stretch my legs, I began to step off the bike when I felt a sharp, searing pain. Jumping with a yelp, I looked down at my left calf. What I saw was a raw patch with a piece of melted skin hanging off. Unwittingly, I had placed my leg squarely against the hot muffler. I was dumbfounded.

Staring at my injury, I slowly stated the obvious. "I guess I burned my leg."

Just one glance told Shya the whole story and sent him into action.

"Ice!"

The station didn't have any, so Shya sprinted off in an attempt to locate some. But there wasn't even a corner store or local coffee shop open for business. Stuffing a five into the attendant's hand, we rushed to make our way to Jones Beach, which seemed the closest place to go for ice. The wind on the burn was wicked. The air, which had only moments before seemed to spell freedom, now brought fire with its touch. The shock of the initial injury having worn off, I was now crying freely as I held Shya tightly around the middle and we sped to the beach.

By the time we pulled into the parking lot, I was beside myself with pain. Shya pulled up to the curb, hopped off, and grabbed our things. He gave me a hand as I limped over to a nearby concession stand where surely they had ice and some cooling relief.

I stood shakily nearby, almost mute with pain, and Shya ran up to the nearest person behind the counter.

"Quick, I need some ice. My girlfriend has been badly burned!"

I turned to show her my leg, which by now looked white and red and raw, thoroughly seared, and nauseating to look at. Sometimes when I see a person with a particularly nasty-looking abrasion, I get a sensation that shoots into my stomach or groin as I can imagine the pain. Had I been a casual observer, I am sure the sight of my leg would have brought a similar rush.

In one fluid movement the manager scooped a large cup of ice and said, "Sorry about your leg. Be sure to come back if you need more."

Wrapping the cubes in a napkin, I hesitantly pressed the cold to my injury. The touch of the paper was agonizing, and I realized I was shaking. As the ice began to melt, dripping down my leg, I finally found some numbing relief.

Eventually, Shya and I shared a plate of greasy french fries and ketchup, and I realized that I wasn't going to get to lie on my towel and sun myself that day. The idea of sand on my calf made me cringe. So we sat at the table, people watching and sipping a giant Coke and looking at the tantalizing ocean in the distance as we waited for the chill to take over and quiet the fiery spot on my left calf.

Finally, with the pain mostly under control, we decided to cut our losses and head for home. I refilled my napkin with bits of ice for the ride back to the city, and we began to make our way to the parking lot and our trusty steed, Old Blue, who was stoically awaiting our return.

There was only one problem with this plan. By the time we got to the bike, the pain in my leg had reflared tenfold. Each stride had become agonizing as the calf muscle flexed and bunched under the wound. It felt as if the skin was drying and cracking, and the throbbing that had mostly been held at bay by the icy compresses began to pound in earnest.

I sat down on the curb by the bike, pressed the compress to my leg, laid my head on my knees, and began to cry. I could tell my shoulders were lurching up and down with my sobs, but I couldn't control them any more than the meager bit of ice I had left in the napkin could control the intense throbbing. Just the idea of wind rushing across the open sore on the way home was enough to cause my sobs to deepen.

Shya sat beside me and took my free hand in his. Gently, his voice came in my ear, "Ariel, let's look at the pain together."

"NO! Don't touch it!" I cried, hunching protectively over the leg.

"Ariel," he continued quietly, "I don't want to touch it. Let's just examine the pain. OK?"

Hesitantly, I raised my head. I looked into his intense hazel eyes and slowly nodded as the tears streamed down my face.

"Trust me," he said.

As I gazed into his eyes, I had no doubt that I could trust this man. There was a calm in him—a steadiness that seemed to translate itself to me. It calmed some of the hysteria of my sobs into sniffles and hiccups. Still the tears silently slid down my cheeks because, while I wished I could crawl out of my skin and leave it behind, the pain in my leg was still real and agonizing and no amount of wishing it would be different seemed to change the situation.

"Ready?" he asked. I nodded, and so we began.

I didn't know at the time that we were going to perform magic. All I knew was that we were going to look at the pain, whatever that meant.

"OK, Ariel. Close your eyes and look at the pain with your mind's eye. If the pain in your calf had a color, what color would it be?"

That was easy. "Fiery red."

"Fine. Now, if it could hold water, how much water would it hold?"

I pictured in a flash the swimming pool from my alma mater, Mt. Hood Community College, so I told Shya it would hold as much water as "an Olympic-sized swimming pool."

"OK," he said. "How about now? If it had a shape what shape would it be?"

"Flat, kind of oval with rough and bumpy razor-sharp edges sticking out."

"Good, Ariel. You are doing just fine. Take a look at the pain now and on a scale of ten, ten being excruciating and zero being no pain, what number does the pain in your leg have now?"

"Twenty-three!"

I knew the number I gave him was off the scale, but I didn't care. My leg hurt and it hurt darn bad.

"All right. And if it had a color right now, Ariel, what color would it be?"

As I looked the color had changed. It was now an orangey red with flaring spots of more intense color, so that is what I reported. As the process continued, Shya kept directing me to look at the shape and color and scale and volume of water the spot on my leg held now and now and now. Each moment became a separate jewel in time, not to be gotten away from or ignored—nor to be compared to the moment preceding it—they became individual facets to be investigated and described.

An amazing thing happened. The color changed through yellows to blues and greens, and finally turned white. The volume of water shrank, to a gallon, a quart, a cup, and

Each moment became a separate jewel in time, not to be gotten away from or ignored—nor to be compared to the moment preceding it—they became individual facets to be investigated and described.

eventually was to be measured only in teaspoons and then drops. Even as the shape shrank to be the size of the head of a pin, so did the numbers I assigned to the pain's intensity recede to two and then one.

We had done it! We had looked the pain of the situation squarely in the eye, and it had disappeared, dissolved, transformed. I felt a profound sense of relief. And it wasn't just a parlor trick either. Gingerly I got up and walked a bit. The pain had somehow been lifted even more than when it had been chilled by two giant soft drink cups' worth of ice. And the sensation didn't even flare up on the ride home, even with the wind wrapping itself around my leg.

Looking again at the Principles of Instantaneous Transformation, in this situation what we did was:

1. Not resist what was, i.e., the pain or the fact that Ariel had been burned. The concept most people hold about pain is that it is static and always the same. This is inaccurate.
2. We looked at the pain moment by moment to see the truth of it in each moment and recognized the pain could only be the way it was.
3. By actually letting the pain be the way it was, it completed itself and disappeared. It is important to note here that we did not look at the pain in order to get it

to shrink or with the intention to get rid of it. Although neither of us wished for Ariel to be in pain, if we had used this seeing the pain in her mind's eye as a method to make it go away, this would have been the First Principle all over again and what we were resisting would have persisted and grown stronger.

In Ariel's story about the burn, we have seen how the Three Principles of Instantaneous Transformation and being in the moment dissolve physical pain. We have also seen how Cecil's emotional pain and guilt regarding his mother's death transformed in an instant. Next let us join Sarah as she discovers how to get control of her upsets, and how a four-year-old boy helped to show her the way.

APPLY THE BRAKES AND BACK OUT
As told by Shya.

Sarah was sitting to our right, and it was clear that she had a burning desire to speak. We were leading one of our Monday evening seminars in Manhattan, and Sarah was radiating her frustration—the subject of which had yet to be revealed.

Ariel must have decided to give her a bit of help, saying, "Who has a question or wants to say something?" Her gaze floated across the sea of faces and landed with a smile on Sarah.

Sarah is an African American woman in her early forties. She has a fiery nature, offset by her natural elegance. She leaped at the chance and jumped to her feet.

"Ariel, Shya," she said, "I'm so frustrated I can hardly stand myself." She waved her hands with a dramatic and slightly humorous flourish.

With mock seriousness I asked, "What happened?" which caused Sarah to chuckle and ratcheted her tension down considerably.

"I keep getting upset! It drives me crazy. And I can't seem to help myself. I go from upset to upset; they keep growing like weeds!"

"Do you drive?" I asked.

"What?" Sarah looked confused. She was just about to tell us the dramatic details of her upset. But she didn't know that repeating those details could very likely restart the cycle of being upset yet again.

"A car. Do you know how to drive a car?"

Slowly she nodded yes. I could tell she was wondering where I was going and what it had to do with being upset.

"Well, if you were driving your car and you made a turn onto a one-way street and discovered that you were going the wrong way, what's the first thing you'd do?"

"Scream!"

The group laughed and Ariel smiled too, as she said, "Let's assume that screaming is not necessary in this situation, OK?"

I asked again, "If you turned onto a one-way street and discovered that you were now pointing the wrong direction, what's the first thing, aside from screaming, you should do?"

"Look behind me."

"Well, if you did that, then you might keep going and hit something."

"Oh, that's true," Sarah said. "I'd stop."

"Right, you'd apply the brakes, and, if possible, you'd back out. Upsets are like that, Sarah. When you start to get upset, just apply the brakes and back out."

Ariel continued, "Many years ago, Shya and I rented a home, and our landlord lived next door. He was a very disagreeable man, and we found ourselves repeatedly upset by his behavior. One very hot summer evening, Shya and I went for a late-night walk. There was no one around since we lived in the country. As we walked up the road we brought our landlord with us . . . in our complaints. He went up the road and down, keeping us company as we found ourselves once again upset by something that had already happened that we had no hope of changing. We were deeply in the upset and complaint compartment in our minds. This is the equivalent of driving down a one-way street in the wrong direction. Right then and there we agreed to back out of that compartment. And you know what? It worked."

Sarah looked thoughtful. This clearly had never occurred to her. A slow smile spread across her face. "Really, do you think I can do that?" and then a moment later, "How do I do that?"

All of us had a good chuckle at that.

"Well, Sarah, when you're complaining, you're saying that things shouldn't be as they are, that the moment isn't perfect."

"But it isn't . . . just look at my hair! In all this humidity it just goes frizzy." She grinned.

"Ah, Sarah," Ariel continued. "You hit upon the key. A full-blown upset is just the tip of the iceberg. If you find yourself rolling from one upset to another, start by looking at those small, seemingly harmless complaints."

Sarah cocked her head to the side. "How do you mean?"

"Let's go back to the Three Principles of Instantaneous Transformation, shall we?" I prompted. "The First Principle is: Anything you resist will persist and grow stronger. Take a small complaint. Any complaint is a form of resistance. The more you complain about your hair, for instance, the more attention you place on it. The more weight it takes on, no pun intended."

Sarah smiled, touched her hair, and nodded.

"Next is the Second Principle of Instantaneous Transformation, which states that you can only be exactly as you are in any given moment. In other words, you can only have the hair you have or be standing where you are right now, and you couldn't be in any other place being any other way, really. Of course each of us has a fantasy of how things could be or perhaps should be different, but, Sarah, you can only be here exactly as you are right now."

Sarah still looked a little confused, but she was relaxing. She was no longer poised on the top of the slide preparing to jump down that slippery slope into an upset.

Ariel took over from there. "Sarah, the Third Principle of Instantaneous Transformation is: Anything that you allow to be, without judging it or trying to fix it, will complete itself and cease to dominate you and your life."

"Let me explain further," I said. "If you find yourself complaining or upset, that is the only way you can be in that moment. Let's pretend that my fingers are a digital camera, and as I snap my fingers I take a picture of your image. Is it possible that in that instant you could have been seated?"

"No, of course not!" she said with a breathless grin. Sarah was engaged in this conversation and her upset was gone.

"Well, can you possibly not be upset when you are?"

"No," she said, a bit more slowly this time. "If I am upset, that is how I am. I may have a fantasy of things getting better, but it is obvious that things are the way they are, especially when I am upset. But I don't like it and I want to change it," she said, stamping her foot.

We all had to laugh as Sarah was actually happily outlining her dilemma.

"OK, Sarah, not liking it takes you right back to the First Principle: What you resist persists. Of course, if the Second Principle is true, as we have seen that it is, then if you don't like being upset, then you can only not like being upset. You can only be you, however you are, in any given moment. Luckily, there is a Third Principle of Instantaneous Transformation: Anything you allow to be exactly as it is will complete itself and stop dominating you."

"OK," she said. "I am beginning to see."

"Your earlier solution about screaming when you see that you are going down a one-way street in the wrong direction was more than just a good joke; it is really how you approach these upsets. When you find yourself upset, you complain and scream in your thoughts. You don't realize that you can simply skip that step. It is possible that you can just stop, apply the brakes, and back out of that compartment."

At this point our friend Andy, who was seated to our left, stood up and asked, "May I add something?"

"Of course, Andy." Ariel said.

"Sarah, I have a little boy, Alex. He is four years old. He had a temper tantrum the other day because he didn't want to brush his teeth. He was mad at me and said that he didn't understand why I got to make all of the rules. He wanted to make some rules. I calmly told him that brushing his teeth wasn't my rule—it was the dentist's rule. After Alex brushed his teeth, I sat on the floor with him and we talked. I talked about this upset he had been experiencing. 'Alex,' I said, 'do you know that feeling you get when you are upset, how it comes over you?' He nodded yes, so I said, 'Well, then, if you want to make a rule, if you want to be in charge, you can tell it no! Tell it to go away.' Alex looked thoughtful, and then his whole face lit up and he shouted, 'I can tell it to go to jail!'"

We all laughed as Andy finished his tale. "This was a four-year-old's funny version of saying no, of applying the brakes and backing out of going down a one-way street in the wrong direction. I have watched him wrestle with his feelings since then. Sometimes he even shouts out loud and we laugh as he learns that he is in charge, not the upset."

There was a smattering of applause, and Sarah smiled as she and Andy both sat back down. From her chair she piped up, "I guess I can learn a thing or two from a four-year-old! Thank you, Andy. Thank you, Ariel and Shya. I am excited to see what happens from here."

"Are you upset now?" I asked.

Sarah sat up a little straighter in her chair as she replied, "Not at all. My car is traveling in the right direction, and I am at the wheel."

4

PREJUDICES

*E*ach of us has mechanical behaviors that follow us through life. If you want to dissolve those unconscious restrictions that limit you and your ability to experience well-being on a moment-to-moment basis, a good place to start is to honestly look at your prejudices. False beliefs, ignorance, and prejudice keep individuals locked in repeating patterns. Sometimes it is even prejudice against prejudice that keeps people stuck. Have you ever heard someone emphatically state, "I am not prejudiced!"? Inherent in that statement is the subtext "Only 'bad' people or 'stupid' people are prejudiced and surely I am not one of those." If you judge your prejudices as wrong instead of simply being aware of them, you will be putting on blinders. You won't readily see the truth about how you mechanically operate in your life because you won't want to be wrong. This path leads to ignorance.

To deny that each and every one of us has prejudices is akin to pretending that we don't breathe. How about the statement "Wow, what a beautiful figure!" In Bali many women dream of having a curvaceous bottom and prominent hips, while in the United States women work diligently to trim those hips and that derriere. Have you

Webster's Dictionary defines *enlightenment* as "to be free of ignorance, false belief, or prejudice."

ever considered that your picture of the ideal woman or ideal man might be a culturally based prejudice that could inhibit your ability to relate? Perhaps it hasn't occurred to most that thinking someone has "beautiful" eyes can be a prejudice in and of itself.

A prejudice, according to the dictionary, is simply "an opinion formed beforehand or without knowledge or thought." If you want to discover your own doorway to enlightenment, if you want to instantaneously transform, you have to be willing to become aware of your cultural and familial beliefs and prejudices, acknowledge them, and then have the courage to find what is actually true for you by taking off your blinders.

TAKING OFF THE BLINDERS

Part of the process of freeing yourself from blindly following your enculturated way of viewing life and releasing yourself from your prejudices and preconceived notions is to discover exactly what you are resisting. For example, if you choose a path in opposition to a person, such as a parent, or a group, such as a church, you are in effect resisting them, and in so doing, you narrow the way you can behave in your life to one option. This option is to be "not like them." Rather than having infinite possibilities and life choices available, your behavior becomes constricted to the polar opposite of what you are resisting. Ever heard of the terms "dead set against" and "dead right"? It is not surprising that both of these phrases use the word *dead*. When one is set in a position that allows for no other possibility, it kills off aliveness and spirit, wonder and creativity.

If you want to discover how to neutralize your prejudices, get interested in what they are. Employ awareness, your ability to neutrally observe, because if you think your prejudices are bad or wrong, you won't want to see them. You can create a game where you pretend you are a scientist or an anthropologist discovering the way that a particular culture functions or operates. Don't take anything that you discover personally. It isn't personal. Many of your prejudices were absorbed from the culture you grew up in, and unconsciously you have internalized these cultural values without the benefit of seeing whether they are honestly true for you.

It is even probable that some of your strong desires and important goals are simply culturally determined prejudices. "Not possible!" you might say. But are you sure your aspirations are wholly your own?

Here is an example: Have you ever lain in bed at night dreaming of accomplishing an important goal? Think back   did this goal ever have anything to do with having your teeth filed? By the age of thirteen did you fervently dream of participating in a ceremony during which a priest filed down your canine teeth so that they are even with your front teeth? Did you ever think that a tooth-filing ceremony like this would signal to the world that you are finally an adult? Do you believe that if you haven't undergone this particular rite of passage that you will never fully be successful in life and that you will never marry well? We have met just such a man in Bali, Indonesia. Wayan was so embarrassed that he had yet to have his teeth filed that he held himself as a failure in life and rarely smiled because he didn't want people to see his shameful teeth. When he was thirty his family eventually raised the money to belatedly hold this ceremony so that Wayan could finally be considered a man.

This is an example of a culturally derived prejudice. Anybody in that culture who hasn't had this ceremony is looked down upon as if he or she is a lesser person. Wayan as a member of this society measured himself against that standard.

If you want to discover what your prejudices are, simply start by being aware—noticing your likes and dislikes. Notice your dreams and aspirations too. We are not suggesting that all of your dreams are prejudices, nor that you need to do anything about what you discover. Neutral observation is enough to dissolve the limiting nature of your prejudices. You can also bring your attention to the automatic nature of your mind and your thought processes while having a sense of humor about what you see. Don't forget that prejudices were most often set in place before you had the opportunity to have full reason or thought.

It all goes back to the Principles of Instantaneous Transformation. It is all about seeing without judging what you see. It is about noticing how you may automatically assume that a doctor or a CEO is a man or that a fashion model is a woman.

Prejudices are automatic assumptions of truth or fact. They often show up like shadowy half images playing in the background, of which you normally aren't aware. For instance, a woman named Beth came to one of our evening groups. She was talking about her day and all the things she had been handling. Beth is the president of her company, and she spoke about having to leave work to let the plumber into her home to fix a leak under the sink. Everyone was surprised when she said, "So when the plumber rang the doorbell, I was there to let *her* in." It was a jolt that Beth's plumber was a woman. In people's minds, as they followed her story, they assumed the plumber was a man, even though people conceptually know that it is possible for a woman to hold a job that has been traditionally held by a man. Your mind categorizes and automatically fills in the details that it expects. If you have a sense of humor about what you see, rather than berating yourself for being "prejudiced," these automatic ideas, which were formed in the past, no longer have to determine how you live your life.

COMING FULL 'IRCLE

What if you are living your life perfectly? What if things that you think are failings on your part are not really failings at all? As a child you absorbed information from your environment perfectly, learning wholeheartedly even when your brain could not yet discern truth from fiction nor apply reason and thought.

Our friends Amy and Andy have a beautiful little boy, Alex. You were introduced to Alex as a four-year-old earlier. In that previous chapter, he was learning to control his upsets by telling them to go to jail. We were privileged to be at the hospital when Alex was born and have watched him on his journey from infancy to childhood.

When Alex was fifteen months old he discovered circles. For some time, Alex was like an investigative reporter, on the hunt for anything round that he could point out with glee to his parents and anyone who would listen. "'Ircle!" Alex would shout. It seemed that, while his brain was able to identify the shape, his mouth could not yet form the *S* sound at the beginning of the word. So instead of being surrounded by circular shapes, Alex's world was inhabited by "'ircles."

Alex could find 'ircles anywhere—the balloon motif around the ceiling at the doctor's office, a clock face, a ball. The MasterCard logo once sent Alex into a frenzy when he realized it had two overlapping 'ircles. It often surprised his parents that round shapes, even when simply part of the background, could be spotlighted by Alex's nimble mind. Amy and Andy found the passion their son had for 'ircles endearing. They did, however, from time to time feel concerned that Alex couldn't pronounce the word correctly. They could only hope that sooner or later Alex would be able to fix his earlier mistake in pronunciation when his ability to speak caught up with his powers of observation.

One day, while casually leaning on the doorframe watching his son play, Andy had a stunning revelation. Alex was on all fours, rolling a big yellow school bus, one of his favorite toys, back and forth. On the side of the bus were four shapes: a triangle, a square, a heart, and a circle. Plopping on his behind, Alex pushed the triangle, and when the button was depressed, an electronic voice exclaimed,

"Triangle!" When Alex hit the square, the voice called out, "Square!" And then he pushed the big round button and the machine hollered, "'ircle!"

Astounded, Andy came into the room, knelt by his son, and pushed the button. Again the toy faithfully repeated, "'ircle!" Alex could make the *S* sound. It was not his mistake. He had learned perfectly, and with passion, to say 'ircle instead of circle from a defective toy.

All of us learned how to behave and relate from things we put together as youngsters or by ideas we absorbed from our environment. But that was before we had the ability to discern whether or not we were getting complete or accurate information.

As you go through life, it is very easy to blame your parents or teachers or environment and say they were bad role models or deficient in some way. But stop and think. Those people you seek to blame also learned and absorbed from their environments without their young minds being able to discern truth from fiction or apply reason and thought.

Just the way Andy discovered the defective audio in his son's toy, you can also discover how you function. Casually lean on the doorframe of your life and observe how you operate without judging what you discover. You will be instantaneously empowered to include small details that you missed as a child. If you can treat yourself with humor, love, and respect, much like you would a young child who is learning from his or her environment, you will reclaim your wholehearted nature and passion for living. When you allow yourself to come full 'ircle, and discover the art of self-observation without self-reproach, it will have a profound impact on your well-being.

BEING RIGHT VERSUS BEING ALIVE

It is virtually impossible to treat yourself with humor, love, and respect if you are living from a point of view where you are being "right" that someone or something has damaged you in your life, or if you are determined to prove that another person is in the "wrong."

As an analogy, you could say that there are two houses in which to live, but you can dwell in only one of them. There is the Right house, and there is the Alive house.

In the Right house, you get to be "right," righteously right—not necessarily correct, but always right. In other words, your point of view is the only possible one and anybody who doesn't agree with your perspective is "wrong."

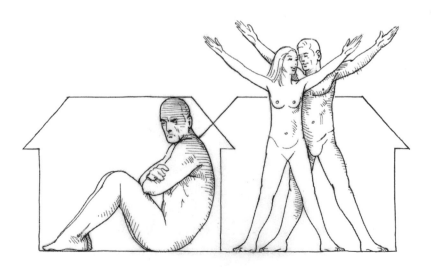

In the Alive house, you get to experience love, health, happiness, full self-expression, satisfaction, relationship, and so on.

To live in either of these houses, you must pay rent. In order to live in the Right house, the rent you have to pay is giving up the experience of love, health, happiness, full self-expression, satisfaction, relationship, and so on.

In order to live in the Alive house, you have to give up being "right." That is all it takes to have an alive, joyous life. You must simply be willing to let go of the need to have the point of view that you are right dominate all aspects of your life. This is especially challenging when you are, in fact, correct. But if you have to prove another is wrong, even if you win, you lose. Something inside you is less alive.

When you defend your point of view and refuse to see any other point of view, you are locked in a right/wrong dynamic whose outcome can only be the loss of your sense of well-being and aliveness. Again, what it costs to maintain that position of being right about your point of view is the experience of loving and being loved, the experience of well-being and full self-expression, the experience of being in relationship with others. It costs you your sense of happiness. Why it costs these things is that those experiences, metaphorically speaking, are on a toggle switch, like a light switch, and they are either on or off. There is no rheostat or dimmer. You cannot simultaneously hold a position of self-righteousness and experience well-being. In order to maintain your point of view, you must disregard all other points of view. You must exclude them and push them away. When you say no to anything that challenges your viewpoint on any particular subject, it restricts the channel or conduit through which experience flows. In order to experience love and well-being, relaxation or openness is required, which defending a point of view precludes.

MADDY'S STORY

We once met a woman in her mid-sixties, Maddy, who was "right" about being a victim of her insensitive mother and a whole host of people throughout her life, mostly women. She told many stories about how she had been scolded and chastised, especially by her parents and teachers but also by perfect strangers. As we came to know Maddy we realized that she was unaware that she herself set up situations where people were likely to speak aggressively to her, which she would then perceive as scolding. For instance, Maddy was not particularly stable on her feet, yet she had a habit of teetering at the top of stairs or other potentially dangerous places while lost in conversation, much to the annoyance of those who cared about her. We noticed that when her friends suggested that she move away from the edge she would stare at them blankly, as if they were speaking in a foreign language. Occasionally someone resorted to speaking forcefully to get her attention when in fear for her safety. Maddy's perspective on life became self-fulfilling, and her behavior and subsequent lack of responsibility reinforced the idea that she was often chastised. But Maddy also interpreted censure from others where none existed. If someone said, "Wow, you look nice today," she would insist that this was an indirect way of telling her that she didn't look nice yesterday. She was so determined to be right about her point of view that it precluded any sense of well-being, it limited her ability to have friends in general, and at age sixty-five she had yet to have a romantic relationship.

Maddy's example may sound quite extreme, but if you pay attention you will see how you diminish your own capacity for love, health, happiness, and full self-expression. Just look at your tendency to complain. Anything that you find yourself complaining about, you are also being "right" about and you shut off your aliveness.

TONY'S STORY

Here is another example. One evening we were invited to an impromptu dinner with a rather large group of friends who were spending the night at a hotel. On the way to the restaurant a fellow named Tony started complaining. Tony groused that the last time he had eaten at this particular establishment, it had taken a long time to be served. But at this point the dinner was already arranged. Tony hadn't wanted to take part in setting up the arrangements but was more than happy to criticize once nothing could be done to change the plans.

As it turned out, it did indeed take some time for everyone to order and be served as there were close to thirty people in the group. Folks relaxed into the situation and chatted with the people around them. As the evening progressed, Tony forgot his objections and had fun socializing.

Several hours later, after having consumed the appetizers and main dishes, the general consensus was that people were willing to forgo dessert in order to pay the bill and head back to the hotel. As the bill was being settled, Tony picked up his complaints and protested loudly, "But I would have liked to have dessert." His friends and especially the fellow who organized the outing weren't able to placate him. In that moment, Tony lost all sense of the people around him and showed no regard for how his complaints affected his friends. He was no longer happy. He was not experiencing satisfaction. He lost his affinity for others—but he was right. So people entertained the idea of changing their plans and staying, but it was already late and they realized that it would be another hour or two, at best, if they ordered desserts and the bill needed to be refigured.

At this point, Tony's friends stepped forward, offering special cookies and goodies that they had stashed in their rooms back at the hotel, but he was determined to be right. "No," he said. "That's not the point. I wanted dessert."

There are times when your life does not go the way you would prefer. What you do with this is up to you. You can be *right* or you can be *alive*. As with Tony, what you resist persists, grows stronger, and dominates your life (First Principle), even though things can only be exactly as they are in this moment (Second Principle). With awareness, a nonjudgmental seeing (Third Principle), you can recognize your preferences and see your complaints and include them but not have to live through them or voice them. Your mind is a machine that is capable of disagreeing with the best of circumstances, but with awareness you can disengage from the internal mental commentary and experience being alive day in, day out, not just when circumstances happen to be easy.

CARMEN'S STORY

Sometimes people absorb ideas about themselves that over time they unwittingly keep proving to be right. With awareness, you can see those old limiting mental structures and not have to be run by them. Such was the case with Carmen, who was born partially paralyzed on one side. Her left leg and arm are significantly weaker than the right, and she struggled her whole life to strengthen the muscles while hiding her infirmity from those around her. Carmen's life became an endless stream of disappointments as she sorted everything into lists of things she could and could not do. The things she thought she could do were narrowly defined, while activities in which she should not or could not participate were an ever-growing list. It had not occurred to Carmen to challenge the assumptions she had made about her abilities. It had not entered her mind to challenge advice given to her by well-meaning physicians, physical therapists, and family members as they did their best to shield her from hurt. By the time Carmen became an adult, she lived in a cocoon of limitations that were effectively cutting out her aliveness.

During one of our Costa Rican Self-Discovery Adventures, Carmen spoke about her affliction, and during the discussion another participant, named Allen, spoke up. Allen has severe asthma, extreme allergies, and scoliosis, which doctors told him would lead to life in a wheelchair by the time he was twenty. Now in his mid-thirties, Allen described how he was healthier than he had ever been before. He told everyone how he had become a professional singer and dancer. His enthusiasm for life had supported him in pursuing things that, according to the professionals, "couldn't be done." According to recent tests, Allen told us, his allergies to pet hair, pollen, dust, and mold were some of the most severe his allergist had ever seen, yet his doctor was mystified as to why Allen didn't exhibit problems in his day-to-day life.

Allen hadn't pursued his dreams of being a performer to prove that the doctors were "wrong"; he just went ahead expressing himself into life while still being attentive to the needs of his body. He was careful to tell Carmen that he was not suggesting that she did not have a physical challenge but rather that what this condition meant was open to interpretation. Perhaps, he suggested, she was living out of inaccurate ideas, which were now prejudicing her ability to live her life fully. He encouraged her to look newly rather than live out of the label of "handicapped."

This conversation presented a new possibility, creating an opening for Carmen. She heartily thanked Allen, and you could see that he had given her food for thought.

One evening, later in the week, we quietly watched Carmen as people planned an activity that normally she would never have allowed herself to consider—a canopy tour. This tour is an adventure into the rainforest, seeing the jungle from the treetops, which requires climbing and wearing a harness to slide down cables suspended between platforms high above the jungle floor. We knew in that moment that

Carmen had a choice. She could be "right" about her affliction or she could allow herself to be supported by others.
People who had been on this tour before encouraged her,
since they knew it was well within her capabilities. In order
to join in, she needed to give up her point of view about her
limitations and discover her greatness. She could be right
or she could be alive. As plans were being made, suddenly
Carmen's face lit up with delight at the possibility that she
could participate. Instantly she looked younger and more
vibrant and alive. In that moment, her old limiting ideas
no longer held sway. Carmen's blinders came off, and she
saw the truth, her truth. She wholeheartedly wanted to go
and she was indeed capable. In that moment, Carmen realized that she could do more, much more than she had been
allowing herself. She went on that canopy tour with her
friends and had the time of her life.

THE DEATH OF THE PAST

Most of us have a strong attachment to our story of what
happened in the past, and often we don't recognize how
powerfully this story affects our lives. We are attached not
only to memories of the good times, but also to memories
of the bad times. We fear that if we let go of it all, we will
be less interesting or we won't know who we are anymore—
that something important about us will die.

We once led a workshop at a retreat center in Phoe-
nicia, New York. A young woman introduced herself to
the group: "My name is Mary. I am twenty-six years old, I
have six million dollars, and people are only interested in

me for my money." With this statement, Mary ensured that her complaint would continue because she'd corrupted the present moment with her story. She ensured that those in attendance would hold her the same way that others had by giving them information from the past that could only influence the way in which they interacted with her.

In order to move into our full potential as human beings, we have to let go of what we already know. Most people hold on to what they know and their idea of who they are, complaints and all, for fear they won't survive. What keeps us stuck in the same old stories is that we never let them complete themselves. Waking up, the ability to live in the moment, is a dying of the old—the old way in which we perceive our lives. We have to let go of our attachment to the past in order to discover who we are in this moment.

MEMORIES: FACT OR FICTION

Let us investigate memories for a moment. A common misconception is that our memories accurately represent past events. But in fact they are simply recordings of those events made from the point of view of the person we were at that time.

Hasn't your life expanded in the past five or ten years? If the answer to this question is "yes," then even your truest memories were set in place by a more limited version of yourself, and, like a tape that has been repeatedly played, all memories distort over time. Your memories of who you were and what you were capable of corrupt this moment. These ideas, built at a time when you were indeed less expanded, form a film, overlaying the moment with a version of you that is at best limited and often completely false. Certainly our childhood memories of disagreements or injustices we experienced were, at best, originally told in that child's voice from a young and immature perspective. Each retelling of this story, to ourselves in our thoughts or out loud to others, has been modified by the point of view we possessed at the time of the retelling.

Following are two examples of how our memories can actually be misinterpretations of a child's mind, as told from Shya's point of view. The first is from Shya's own childhood, and the second example he witnessed as an adult.

The Spalding Moon

I was four when my father made the moon. We were playing catch. It was late. The 7:20 had arrived in Far Rockaway, and my father had caught a ride from the station with old Joe Benson. I was waiting in the yard, grass tickling my bare feet. In my hand I clutched the moon—a small pink Spalding rubber ball.

"Daddy, Daddy," I shouted before he even had a chance to catch his breath. "Play catch with me! Please, puh-lease," I begged.

Even then my dad had a cherubic face. It crinkled in pleasure, the weight of the day falling from his shoulders. His daily paper dropped to the stoop.

"OK, Shya, give me the ball and run over there."

I handed him the ball, gave him a quick hug around the waist, and dashed to the edge of the lawn. He tossed me a few. I hardly caught any, but my enthusiasm sparkled like the early stars edging their way through the chiseled blue. The sun had set, its fire all but extinguished, and then my dad, who was my hero and capable of anything, produced a miracle. He pitched that pink Spalding rubber ball high into the evening sky and that was when he made the moon. Yes, my father had thrown up a Spalding moon. I was mesmerized. Long after my father disappeared into the house I sat on the stoop and gazed at what he had created.

I believed with all my heart that my father made the moon. It was years before I was disabused of this notion. Sometimes I look at my life and have to simply shake my head as I see that there is the story and then there is the obvious. As a child I told myself many things that appeared true to me at the time that indeed were just my imaginings and grossly inaccurate.

The Boy and the Well

Once I built a house in Maine. It was way back in the woods, and you needed to have a four-wheel-drive vehicle to get to it. I built my home on the foundation of an old farmhouse that had existed there many years before.

One day an old man came down the road and said, "I used to live here many years ago when I was just a boy. I would really like it if I could look around. May I?"

I said, "Sure," and he seemed happy that I would let him see his old childhood home.

"There was a great big cellar hole that was maybe fifty feet by fifty feet—it was huge," he told me.

So we went to take a look at the cellar over which I had built my house. The real dimensions were about twenty feet by twenty feet. The old man was shocked.

"This couldn't be! This is so small. Where I grew up was much bigger. It was huge!"

As we climbed the cellar stairs into the light, the man was shaking his head in disbelief.

"There was a well," he said next. "It was at least forty or fifty feet deep."

> If you believe your version of the past you will be living your life built on lies.

There was only one well on the property. I'd had a hard time cleaning it out when I first arrived. I had to dig out mud, old leaves, and debris to clean it down to the bedrock. I took him to the well. Actually, the depth was only eight or nine feet.

To a child, eight or nine feet can look like fifty feet. But it is just a distortion from a child's point of view. The man's memory of the well was how it looked to him as a child. His view of it as an adult was a totally different perception.

False Memories

Recent studies have conclusively shown that false memories can be remembered even more clearly than actual ones.

At Western Washington University, scientists conducted an experiment where researchers told test subjects that they would be asked a series of questions about events from their childhood. The answers would be compared with their family members' memories of the same events.

Here is the catch. Unbeknownst to the test subjects, the investigators asked about an event that had, in fact, never happened. The researchers asked about a time when the participant had, as a child, been to a wedding reception and spilled the punch bowl on the mother of the bride. Initially, none of the participants recollected this incident.

Later, the same subjects were interviewed again. Surprisingly, now many recalled this fictitious event. At this time, some of the participants even "remembered" specific details about the bogus episode.

Researchers have also found that false memories can be created by combining an actual memory with a suggestion made by someone.

Reading about these studies explained certain experiences the two of us have had with our own clients. For example, one of our clients, Tom, the president of a family-owned business, told us that as a child he had a demanding father who regularly humiliated him. He cited as an example the time his father removed the lawn because he felt that Tom had not done a thorough enough job. When we discussed this incident further, Tom realized that his father, who was a heart surgeon, was a very precise man. Tom saw that his dad had not intended to embarrass him but had simply wanted the yard to meet his standard. With his adult eyes, Tom realized that his father's standards were not unreasonable. Actually, he as a ten-year-old, not really wanting to mow the lawn in the first place, had done a less-than-satisfactory job. Subsequently, Tom, who had been estranged from his father, made overtures to reconcile their relationship. In so doing, he discovered that his father was much nicer and more tolerant than he remembered him to be. In fact, he was a great man, and Tom shared many of his traits.

Now enter Tom's brother, Jim. Jim worked for the family enterprise in a different country. We were called in for a consultation when the brothers met at the corporate headquarters. During the conversation, we were surprised to hear Jim relate the same story about mowing the lawn and his demanding, humiliating father as if it had happened to him. He told the story with the same intensity, sentence structure, and cadence as Tom's version. It was so amazingly similar that we questioned both of them about their stories. What we uncovered was that neither brother had an exact recollection of the event. In fact, the story had been related to them by their eldest sister, who had "seen it all." Until that moment, it never occurred to the brothers that their whole attitude about their father had been shaped to fit their sister's point of view. They had "remembered" what she had told them over time as if it were their own experience.

The classic film *Rashomon*, directed by Akira Kurosawa, explores similar themes. This Japanese movie from the early 1950s depicts an incident that takes place between a samurai, his wife, a brigand, and a woodcutter. These four characters live through the same event together. Yet each person's story supports his or her point of view and memory of what happened. Eventually, the viewer finds out what actually transpired, and the truth is vastly different from each participant's version. Our memories are biased by our agendas and points of view. If we hold our memories as The Truth, let them define us, and allow them to filter the way we experience reality, we will surely be misguided.

5

INSTANTANEOUS
TRANSFORMATION

*A*s we saw in the example of Ariel's burn, awareness can dissolve physical pain. Emotional distress can disappear in an instant also, as was the case with Cecil when he suddenly realized that he could not possibly have been with his mother at the time of her passing, releasing him from years of guilt. In these two examples, prior to having an Instantaneous Transformation, both Ariel and Cecil were aware of their pain and were originally powerless to stop it. Instantaneous Transformation can also spontaneously occur in areas of our lives that we never thought to look at before.

Events from our past are threads that we have woven forming the tapestry we call our lives. We all assume that our interpretations of these events are correct and that the conclusions we have drawn from them are true and accurate. Yet obviously our interpretations of life's events are not always correct. In Shya's example of the Spalding moon, his mistaken thought that his father "made" the moon was basically humorous and harmless, something that naturally fell by the wayside along with other childhood myths like Santa

Claus or the tooth fairy. In the example of the man revisiting his childhood home, it had never occurred to him that his memory of looking down the well had been colored by his immature perspective. In his case, the misinterpretation could be seen as simply amusing. But sometimes unexamined, false interpretations of an event create a faulty platform on which we build our entire lives. Fortunately, with awareness, a myth can be seen for what it is and the truth can be revealed in an instant, resulting in a transformational shift. Being in the moment can shine a bright light on old erroneous ideas and create the basis for a wholly new existence.

The following is just such an example, told from Ariel's point of view. It illustrates a profound transformation that happened for a young woman who had never conceived that she was following a faulty path she had laid out for herself as a toddler. It takes place in the early 1990s on the island of Bali in Indonesia where the two of us were speakers at a conference. Jody was an attendee at the event who scheduled a private consulting session with us. When she showed up at our room, none of us expected what came next.

JODY'S STORY

It was about four o'clock and the sun shone through the window of our Nusa Dua Beach hotel room. I was glad that we had air-conditioning because I wasn't used to the heat nor the humidity. Although we were in Bali, Indonesia, for the Second Annual Earth Conference, twelve thousand miles away from home, as Jody came into the room, all of that fell away. Hotel rooms have a way of doing that. Some are much nicer than others, but all in all they have an anonymity and an ability to drop out of time. The background, the town, and even the country can all recede, leaving just you. It is almost as if those rooms are empty vessels waiting to be filled with thousands of moments from thousands of lives. I rarely think of them as a sanctuary or a place for a profound healing to take place, but they can be that too.

Jody, a slim woman with curly dark hair streaked with lively gray highlights, was a little nervous when she came in.

"Why did you book a session with us, Jody? What did you want to have happen for you here?" Shya asked once we all were seated.

"I don't know. People have recommended I give it a try, that I will really like it. I have heard that you do different types of sessions, that you speak with people about issues or consult with businesses. But I also heard that you do some amazing pain relief, and, frankly, I am very sore from hauling my luggage around. My bags are really heavy. I don't know what to expect, but I was sort of hoping you could get rid of the pain in my shoulders."

"OK, Jody, let's get out the massage table. You can lie facedown, and let's see what we can do for you."

I knew that what we were about to do would seem like a type of massage, but actually this pain relief technique, which Shya created, is a form of modern-day alchemy. In ancient alchemy, the philosopher's stone was supposed to transmute lead or base metals into gold. Our technique is like the philosopher's stone. As Jody allowed herself to be with the pain and tension in her body, it disappeared—instantaneously.

We chatted and worked the tension out of her muscles, never really going anywhere, just letting her get in touch with what was there. As Jody felt each spot we found, the pain melted away.

About half an hour into the session, Shya pressed on a tight spot in Jody's neck. She seemed to be holding her breath.

"Take a deep breath, through your mouth and up into your chest," I said quietly near her ear. I felt a wave of sadness. "What is it, Jody? Are you seeing something in your mind's eye?"

Jody took a ragged breath. Almost mouthing the words, they were so faint, she said, "It's so stupid. It's so stupid."

I didn't know what she was talking about, but that didn't matter. "It's OK that it's stupid, let yourself feel this spot."

"It's OK to be sad," Shya finished.

Like a baby drawing in a massive breath just before letting out a tremendous wail, Jody sucked in a lung full of air and silently began to sob.

"It's OK, honey, you can make noise if you want to," I murmured into her ear.

I wouldn't be surprised if someone passing by our door heard a young child bawling her eyes out because that was how it sounded to me. Sobs racked her body. We were just there with her. It's funny how good it felt to be with Jody then. It was almost a holy feeling, as if the source of life itself had been touched somehow. Her weeping was the sound of a forgotten soul coming home after having been left outside in the cold for a long, long time.

"What's happening in the picture you are seeing, Jody?" Shya gently prompted again.

"I touched Daddy's cigarettes." The last word melted into another set of sobs that lasted for some time. Eventually, her crying ebbed and Jody began to regain her control.

"It's so stupid!" she said again.

"It doesn't matter if the picture seems stupid to your adult mind, Jody. Don't judge it. For whatever reason, it was important to a younger version of you."

"I touched Daddy's cigarettes."

"OK, how old were you?"

"Maybe eighteen months, something like that."

"OK, then what happened?"

"Well, Daddy slapped my hand. And—and then he died."

This would explain the tears. Shya and I looked at each other. We knew then that it was likely there was more to this emotional puzzle, which Jody hadn't seen yet.

"When did he die? What happened?"

"Well, he slapped my hand and then he had a heart attack about an hour later."

"And what did you think that meant?"

"I . . . I killed him."

Her sobs began anew, but they held less intensity this time. Quietly, we waited for the storm to subside. Eventually, the downpour softened and then petered out. There was a clean quality in the air, as if something had been cleansed, much the way a soaking rain will drench the earth and wash away the dust, leaving things sparkling in its wake.

"Now run the picture again through your mind like a movie, only this time watch it with your adult eyes. Tell us what you see."

As Jody recounted the tale, it had lost most of its emotional intensity.

"My daddy smoked. I can see the package. They were Lucky Strikes. It was in the living room. I reached for them and then," she took a deep breath, "then, Daddy slapped my hand. I knew I had done something terribly naughty. He died right after that, and I thought that my naughtiness did it. I killed him."

"Jody, did you really kill your father? Did you have anything to do with it at all?"

Jody paused for a moment and sighed. "No. No, I didn't. I just thought I did."

A little while later, when Jody sat up, she looked years younger. She perched rather shakily on the edge of the massage table, so we told her to take her time. We didn't want her to rush and get things back together. That memory had been waiting buried for a long, long time. Jody looked as new as the baby she had been all those years ago.

"You guys, that's amazing! I never thought of that before. Ever! How did you do that?"

Shya looked at me and I at him. With a slight smile, we shrugged.

"Actually, Jody, we didn't *do* anything. We just hung out with you and with whatever was happening in your neck. We just sort of tricked you into the moment, and whatever was left over in your body from your childhood surfaced to be looked at and experienced. Sometimes memories seem to be stored in a person's body. By touching a place of tension and allowing you to feel what is there, it can dissolve. In your case, it seems this memory was triggered by the spot in your neck. But we weren't looking for it nor were we trying to get rid of it once you touched upon it."

I sat next to her and took her hand. "How do you feel?"

Jody's gaze turned inward for a moment. "New. I feel new."

We all sat there for a bit, not saying anything, just savoring the silence, the newness, and the richness of simply being alive.

"I have always felt sad. I never knew why before."

"Ahh, Jody," Shya said with a gentle smile. "Don't blame your sadness on what you saw here today. You were just sad, that's all. How are you—do you feel sad now?"

"No. I don't. I feel . . ." She began searching for the right word to describe her state. Things had slowed down for the three of us. "I feel grateful," she said with a smile, "and I feel curiously empty."

We both nodded. We knew this state well. It is as if some secret place deep inside has been holding on to a piece of the past. When this old relic is finally cleared out, it makes space in your heart to experience life anew.

As she stood up, it became clear that her whole body had rearranged itself. Before it was as if she had been protecting a deep hurt. No amount of massage could cause the kind of transformation that happened when she simply let go of her judgment that what she saw and felt was "stupid" and let herself feel what was there in her heart.

Jody fairly toddled her way out into the late afternoon Balinese sun. She looked like she was finding a whole new set of legs on which to stand, and as I saw her making her way quietly down to the ocean, I felt privileged—privileged to be alive and blessed that Jody had let us be a part of her own rebirth.

A NEW REALITY

Part of what was so beautiful about the experience with Jody was that it was unplanned, not a part of some agenda of hers or ours. We didn't think that there was anything wrong with her that needed to be fixed.

We simply were present with her in a way that allowed her to observe herself in a nonjudgmental manner. We acted as catalytic agents and allowed her to get into the moment. And when Jody got into the moment, without judging what she saw, her life transformed.

A therapist attending one of our seminars once told us that it was clear that we had regressed Jody back to her childhood and obviously it had some therapeutic results. Actually, we didn't "do" anything. None of us was expecting to visit Jody's childhood. It just showed up in the moment.

BEING IN THE MOMENT

Our society tells us that our past has molded us into the way we are now. One of the major components that keeps people from experiencing this moment is their attachment to their life story, which generally blames someone or something for how they are today. The common misconception is that there has got to be a good reason for why we are the way we are. But what if there is no reason?

Sometimes people repeat a story for years—"I am an angry person because my mother hit me when I was four"—and retelling the story does nothing to lessen the anger. If you allow yourself to simply feel angry without judging it or blaming it on past circumstances, then the anger will fade and will lose its hold over you.

After her session with us, Jody wrote and published an article detailing her experience and resulting transformation. Once it appeared in a magazine, a wave of people came to us wanting to fix their "screwed-up" childhoods. The majority of these people came wanting to prove that their parents had raised them wrong. It was challenging for them because their desire to be right that their parents were wrong was often actually stronger than the desire to dissolve the "problem."

Looking at your life through a transformational framework is paradoxical. On the one hand, traumatic incidents in your past have affected your life. On the other hand, you can't blame how you are being in this moment on your past.

You can't fix your childhood. It's over—finished. All of those stories you have from growing up, even the good ones, are a distortion of a child's mind anyway. Remember the man who came to look at the cellar hole and the well at Shya's farm in Maine? Well, the visit to his childhood home disillusioned that man. In other words, the illusions that he had held as truths from a child's memory were dispelled.

FORGIVENESS

Now let's look at another fundamental element for transforming your life: forgiving your parents for anything they did wrong or you think they did wrong. Actually, forgiving the past. Since the memories of your childhood are distortions held over time, the past and your childhood and how your parents or siblings related to you becomes irrelevant.

Learning how to forgive your past is a radical departure from working on your history to bring about change. This is where we jump from a psychological framework to an anthropological one. (Again, an anthropologist notates, or neutrally observes, what he or she sees without trying to change what is seen.)

This is also where our attachments to our stories become evident. Over the years, the two of us have seen folks from all walks of life, including those who have survived sexual and physical abuse, discover how to have the traumas of

Forgiveness

1. to give up resentment against or the desire or right to punish; stop being angry with; pardon.
2. to cancel a debt—to make as if the debt never happened.

their past stop holding sway over their lives and life choices made today.

Our minds act as recording devices. They record events as seen by us at the time of the event. Many of our current beliefs were put in place from the point

> Instantaneous Transformation allows you to transcend your bratty nature.

of view of who we were when we were children. If you were to observe, objectively, the lives of children, you would discover that much of their experience is upsetting. As children learn to cope with life's capricious nature, they become the victim of their disappointments, and from that point of view many life strategies are unknowingly set in place. Then as an adult we function through the viewpoint of a child, never thinking to reexamine those life strategies. As a child, standing in line in a supermarket, seeing the displays of gum and candy, we want them. If our parent says no, it feels so unfair from the perspective of a two- or three-year-old, and suddenly we see the parent as an unreasonable tyrant who is arbitrarily dictating our life. The idea that our parents are the enemy is now locked into place, and this decision is reinforced by many other such denials of our wants and desires.

Human beings have survived through their stubborn nature, and each of us has within us a stubborn, bratty little child who wants what it wants. That is how humanity has survived, through this aggressive persistence in holding on to a point of view. It is not necessarily a bad thing. But if unseen and unchecked, that same attribute can become the source of strife, pain, suffering, and the loss of relationship.

Part of the reason most children judge their parents so severely is that it is impossible, by virtue of lack of maturity, to share an adult perspective. Later, when we're grown, our earlier judgments and ways of being are firmly entrenched and rarely investigated.

Behaviors that seem odd or inappropriate when viewed from the outside make more sense when we can step inside the psyche, logic system, and life circumstances of our parents (or any other person).

If you could *be* them, rather than judging them from the outside or looking at them through the assumption that you know who they are, you might discover compassion for how difficult it is to be a human being on planet Earth.

One of the best gifts you can give to yourself and to others is the gift of forgiveness. Here is an example of how a woman named Kathy had an experience that allowed her to spontaneously dissolve years of conflict between herself and her father. We created a game so that she could walk a mile in his shoes. When she began playing, she never anticipated the depth of compassion that she would discover for her dad.

KATHY'S STORY

Kathy, the head of a theatrical school, hired us to come in and lead a seminar for the students about Instantaneous Transformation and living in the moment. The two hundred budding actors were mainly in their mid- to late teens. As part of the seminar we devised an acting exercise designed to free these students from restrictions they were unaware of, which were limiting their abilities to perform, not to mention their abilities to have fulfilling, successful lives. Many of these youngsters were unwittingly living out of a decision to be "independent" or "not like" one or the other of their parents. This decision kept them from having freedom of self-expression. It precluded them from being fully creative. As a result, the actors became tongue-tied, stilted, or less vibrant if a part required them to act in a way that they perceived was like their mother or father.

Here was the game: We had the students close their eyes and see which parent they most resisted. Next we had them open their eyes and act as if they were at a party. They were asked to pantomime having a drink in hand and move about the room and interact with others. Here was the catch: We asked the students to go to the party as if they were the parent they had traditionally resisted the most. It was about stepping into the skin, the reality, the body postures, the sensations, the attitudes, and even the prejudices of that parent. We instructed them that it was important to *be* their mom or dad rather than show the world what was wrong with him or her. In other words, as they moved around as their parents, they were to be believable as that individual rather than a caricature that telegraphed all of the student's childhood complaints.

Kathy decided to play the game too, never expecting to have Instantaneous Transformation, which completed years of dissatisfaction with and complaints about her father. As the exercise started we met many people who were doing their best to act the part of their mom or dad. When Kathy came up to us, here is what happened.

Thrusting her hand out forcefully, in a blustery loud voice she greeted us. "Hi. I'm Ted. My daughter runs this school. I don't like acting much but I suppose she likes it and does a pretty good job."

Her handshake was crushing. We could tell by her manner that she thought Ted was crude, lacking in social skills, and too loud and opinionated. It was obvious from her demeanor that Kathy expected we would find him as annoying as she did. Kathy wasn't yet just *being* her father; she was highlighting his faults.

So we introduced ourselves in return and asked "Ted" what he did for a living.

"Oh, I'm retired now. But I used to be a colonel in the air force, and in World War II I led lots of raids into enemy territory."

"Were you frightened?"

Suddenly Kathy/Ted's face underwent a transformation. The true answer came unbidden to Kathy's mind. In an instant she actually saw her father, and in that moment she became Ted, rather than rehashing a child's interpretation of who he was.

Kathy's face softened as she answered rather quietly, "Terrified. I was terrified each and every mission, but it was my job, my duty."

"And tell us about your wife, Ted."

"She's a beauty. We've been married more than fifty years, you know. Gave me three great kids. Did I mention Kathy? That she runs this school? I am very proud of her."

With this Kathy choked up and moved off to meet others, and the game continued.

At the end of the day, we had a private conversation with Kathy about what she discovered. As she spoke with us, her eyes misted over. We noticed that her entire body had relaxed. Her face was luminous and her gaze direct.

"Ariel, Shya, that little game was so wonderful. I always thought my dad was uncaring, unfeeling, that he was tough and insensitive. I never, ever realized that he was frightened and that his blustery exterior is something he developed to face adversity, give courage to his troops, and to even let my mother feel that she was safe and taken care of. I always resented him and judged him for being an authoritarian, but as I was *being* him I realized that he is actually very shy. Wow! His gruff exterior is just a protective shell. Oh, and I was shocked to realize how much he loves my mom and how proud he is of me. Thank you both. I feel as if I have met my dad for the very first time."

When Kathy fell into the moment and discovered her father anew, she was finally able to see him nonjudgmentally with adult eyes. It was Instantaneous Transformation, and the benefits ranged forward and back throughout time. In other words, Kathy no longer held all of those past memories of how her dad was "unfeeling" as the truth, and her childish interpretations of his actions lost meaning. Her childhood complaints ceased to dominate her experience of him in that moment. The next time she saw her father, she was able to actually see him rather than have the moment colored by her past complaints.

Ideally, we should feel warm toward and close to all of those we care about. But sometimes hurtful things have been done or said that have created a distance, and we have grown apart. It is hard to understand when people we love disappoint or hurt us. Sometimes their actions seem so unreasonable and inexplicable that we find it nearly impossible to let them back into our hearts. And yet most of us feel a longing for closeness.

For Kathy, the game of *being* her dad allowed her to forgive. At other times, it is important to stay open, listen, and bring awareness to your parent's particular set of circumstances.

In 1993, Shya's mother, Ida, passed away. The time prior to and around her death was surprisingly rich and rewarding. It was a time for discovery and forgiveness. It was a passage where secrets were told and puzzles unraveled. We would like to share this precious experience with you as told from Ariel's point of view.

IDA'S STORY

Ida was no longer breathing. The artery in her neck still pulsed steadily, and I leaned in, calmly watching her lips tinge blue. I knew it would only be a few more moments. Shya's mother, Ida, had been in and out of the hospital for some time. At age eighty-four her doctor had likened her heart to a tire that was old and worn; it was ready to blow at any time. Max, Shya's father, had understandably been very upset by that analogy. Although this comparison might have been insensitive, I felt the doctor was trying his best to prepare Max for the inevitable. I am not surprised that I wasn't as upset as Max was by the doctor's comments. Ida wasn't my wife, and I hadn't spent sixty-four years of my life with her.

For more than fifty of those sixty-four years, Max and Ida had been working together. As a young bookkeeper Ida had spotted Max, who was then a young cutter in New York City's garment district. A cutter is someone who lays out the patterns over layers of material and then cuts the shapes to be sewn. On the day Max asked her for a date, I am told she agreed to go out with him provided he would bring her a pattern of one of the hot new spring dresses. Max fulfilled her request, and it was the beginning of a long and fruitful relationship.

I sometimes wonder what Ida did with that pattern. Sewing wasn't one of her strong suits. By the time I met her, she had taken to embellishing sweaters by appliquéing diamond-shaped swatches of material in a contrasting color to the front, bordering the patches with bric-a-brac of yet another color, and then finishing by sewing in a designer label purloined from Max's dress factory. Ida had an amazing array of hats, sweaters, and the like, upon which I am sure Bill Blass, Scaasi, Vera Wang, and Carolina Herrera would have cringed to see their designer labels.

Ida's decline took a number of years. At first it wasn't so obvious. When she was eighty, Ida still worked two days a week in New York City as the bookkeeper at the Max Kane Dress Company where Max made designer dresses and wedding and ball gowns.

The shifts in Ida's health and mental state are frozen in slidelike time segments of factory life. Although from time to time they came and visited us at our home, we most often saw them at what Ida and Max had come to call "the place."

On one such visit, Ida thoroughly surprised us by asking, "What do you need? If you need money for anything, just let me know and I'll help you. Just don't tell Mr. Kane." She always called Max "Mr. Kane" at the factory, even to us.

The offer for money was quite a shock to Shya. Never in his life had she made such an offer. When he was growing up, money had been very tight. The first clothes he ever owned that were not secondhand were bought with money he earned himself at age fifteen. Spartan spending when buying clothes was only the tip of the iceberg when it came to Ida's way with money, but I will get to that later.

So we took Ida up on her offer. With her assistance we were able to purchase our first car. It was a sweet little yellow ten-year-old Volkswagen Rabbit, which was something we really needed but had been unable to pay for on our own. We were very grateful for the help, and we honored her request not to tell Mr. Kane.

Eventually, during some of our weekly visits to the place, Ida would, as usual, chat about how business was and talk about the different orders they had in house. Quite suddenly she would start talking about a designer that Max hadn't worked for in ten or fifteen years, thinking the orders were current news. It was as if the needle on an old record player had mysteriously skipped grooves and gone back to playing a previous song. Time no longer progressed linearly for Ida. We began to be concerned about her ability to keep the books as it seemed to be more and more stressful for her. Around this time, she and Shya had a very frank conversation.

The rows of sewing machines hummed and vibrated in the background as we sat in her little office under the fluorescent light. "Mom, I am concerned about something," he began. "What if you become sick or incapacitated? Who will know about your finances? Does Dad know what stocks you have or where the accounts are held?"

The answer was no. Ida had been very secretive over the years, but stock dividend checks came to the house regularly. She would keep rubber bands around the piles of used envelopes because, she said, "You never know when you might need scrap paper." Since we were at the factory, Ida took a big sheet of pattern paper and drew some grids. As we sat with her, she made a list of assets. It was obvious that much information was missing, but it was a start.

Soon, Ida started staying home most of the time. The city was too far, her health was failing, and she started losing her balance and falling. Luckily, Max was still strong enough to lift her. All the years of working and cutting had kept the five-foot-three man robust. But he began to worry for her safety when he was gone, so he hired daytime help to keep her company and keep her safe.

Ida's physical decline, which had led inexorably to this hospital bed, had been at times graceful and at times difficult and painful. For instance, it was painful for a formerly self-sufficient person to stop driving. No one wanted to tell her to stop, to take away that freedom. Finally, one day she mistook reverse for park and, thinking she had parked the car, got out. The car reversed, the door knocked her over as it rolled backward, and it was time. She never drove again.

She hated giving up the bookkeeping too, but she was no longer able to make the computations. At Ida's insistence, Max brought the work home for her at first, but soon she got agitated and fretted over it, so he stopped and got a bookkeeper in the city. Before long, it was time for another honest conversation. Oh, these talks could be difficult! How does one bring up with a parent, or anyone for that matter, their mortality, their failing health, their diminishing mental capabilities? This is not something most of us are trained to do. I am sure my parents felt similarly when they had to broach subjects that were embarrassing or agitating to me as I was growing up. Yes, the roles were finally and irrevocably reversing. We were now operating as parents, acting in what we hoped was Ida's best interest as she rapidly assumed the role of child.

"Mom, we need to sort out your finances," Shya bravely began on one telephone call. "Where do you keep your stock certificates and records?"

Ida fidgeted and hemmed and hawed, but eventually we determined she kept them at home, in the freezer. This brought to mind funny images such as certificates frozen in blocks of ice and phrases like "cool cash" and "frozen assets." We knew we were out of our depth. It would take someone more knowledgeable than we were to help sort things out.

So we enlisted the aid of our accountant and friend, Josh, to come out with us and raid the fridge.

A week or two later found us at Ida's house, but we discovered the freezer was bare. Had she hidden things? Was this a new game, perhaps of hide and seek? But no, Ida appeared guileless. Maybe she only thought she'd put them in the freezer. It was time to hunt.

When I was young, my sisters and I would sometimes hide something and one or the other of us would look for the concealed object. Then the person who had hidden the item would give feedback as we searched. "You are getting warm, warmer, hotter" and so on, if we moved toward the hiding place, or "You are getting cold, colder, ice cold," as we moved away.

Well, the freezer was pretty warm, but not the actual stashing spot. Next to the freezer was an old brown shopping bag. This bag was hot, red hot. In this bag we found years and years of accumulated financial information.

Sorting through this brown paper safe-deposit box turned out to be a dangerous mission. Ida had unwittingly booby-trapped the bag for would-be intruders. See, Ida didn't see the need to buy paper clips. Working at a clothing factory she had an endless supply of fine, sharp straight pins. Many times Josh did not need to pluck out a record. As he withdrew his hand from this grown-up version of a grab bag, the record would automatically come along, its pin embedded in a finger or thumb.

Old crumbling bits of doilies, linoleum, fabric, and old, old stocks like Studebaker still lived in that bag. There were other bags there too. Suddenly things began to come clear. Envelopes and rubber bands were not the only things Ida had collected. There in those bags, unbeknownst to her children or even Mr. Kane, Ida had amassed a small fortune. Well, that is not quite true. To be honest, the fortune was more than a small one. Max was shocked.

"She still gets upset when I buy Minute Maid orange juice instead of a store brand," was his comment that I remember most.

So a piece of the puzzle had fallen into place and a picture started to emerge. Now I knew why she never wanted us to tell Mr. Kane about those previous gifts. She hadn't wanted him to suspect she had money to spend.

Months later, in the hospital that day, as I sat waiting at her bedside watching her lips grow blue, I knew we were at a passage.

The moment was coming again, and, holding Ida's hand, I leaned directly into her line of sight so that my face was positioned close in front of hers. It was important that she know she was not alone. Here it came, the gasp, the reflexive gripping of my hand as Ida returned from her journey, sucking in a panicked breath as her body, which was not quite ready to relinquish its hold over her, reasserted its need for oxygen.

I had been with Ida for several hours now. She would stop breathing, journey off, and then return with the terror of one who is starved for air. Her system was sending the equivalent of alarms and bells and whistles. *You are suffocat-*

ing! it would scream, and she would return with a start, in fear for her life. I felt no fear for her, and it showed in my expression and demeanor. So I put my face in her path so it would be the first image she would catch sight of. My calm would then infuse her.

See, I knew in my heart that Ida was terrified of dying. I also knew that each trip she was making now was like a trial run, and that my presence could melt her fear and ease her passing. And in so doing I received many gifts. I got to see the wonder in her eyes as she returned. Focusing on my gaze, love suffused her face. Sometimes, upon her reemergence to consciousness, she would repeat the same sentence over and over. I began to see that many of these were unresolved concerns left over from long ago. Others were stories or events of which she was proud and that she needed to share. And I was the vessel, the fortunate recipient of these gifts. Shya was as well, of course, for he was there in the room, but I loved being with Ida this way, so he gave me space.

Clutching my hand, Ida lurched back to this reality. Disoriented for a minute, she tried to rise up to get more air. I am familiar with this feeling. It is not one of my favorites. Sometimes while meaning to swallow I actually inhale my spit instead and my throat closes, feeling as if I can't breathe; it is hard to relax and not panic. But relaxing was exactly what I was training Ida to do.

I am so pleased to see you back, my look said.

Her look had an intensity. *There is something I have to tell you,* it replied.

As I listened as intently as I knew how, she said, "You have no idea what it is like to be dependent on money and then lose it. I swore I would never become dependent on money again!" There was pleading in her eyes. *Don't judge me!* they entreated.

More pieces of the puzzle gently floated into place. Of course many families go through tight times and have to watch their pennies to make ends meet, but with Ida, conserving money had forever been a supreme priority. When Shya was thirteen, his older sister, Sandra, got a lump on her neck. "Just a swollen gland," the doctor said. For six months this "gland" stayed swollen and grew in size, but no more trips to the doctor were scheduled, no second opinions asked for. Doctors cost money, after all. Finally, finally, they went again. But by then it was too late. Sandra had spinal cancer, and she eventually succumbed to the disease, dying at age twenty-four, seven long years later.

The decision to delay further action on Sandra's lump had embittered some family members, but as I sat with this fragile old lady, holding her hand, I realized that at some moment in time when she was young, Ida had sworn to herself a solemn oath to conserve money, however large a sacrifice it might seem. She had made this promise to herself, never even glimpsing what the future might have in store, and she had paid the ultimate price.

"It's not right for a parent to outlive her children," she had told me more than once.

I smiled down at her a tender smile. *I love you. I forgive you. It's all right; you can rest now.*

Soon Ida began to slide in and out of consciousness with more and more ease. Today was not to be the day of her death, but it was coming. I could feel it.

Ten or so days later, Ida was back in Intensive Care. She would not be going home again. By now, Ida was bedridden. Hooked to an IV, with tubes of oxygen in her nose, she sucked air as she apologetically looked up at us as if she was sorry to be causing so much trouble.

I was again in my customary spot by Ida's side, holding her hand. Within a few minutes she started to drift in and out again, her breathing stopping, her neck pulsing, but by now the process was infinitely easier and simpler. Ida's eyes would remain open, her gaze fixed, and she would just go. When she came back, each return was new and fresh and alive. It went something like this:

As Ida regained awareness of her surroundings, Shya said, "Hello, Ida. Did you have a nice journey?"

"Oh yes," she replied with enthusiasm. "It was beautiful!"

She remained smiling, her wrinkled old face and sunken eyes beatific. Then her countenance relaxed and she was away again, her gaze still looking at me, but she was not there. Holding her hand, I waited. By now, Shya was sitting with me and we had our faces pressed side by side so she could see us both when she reemerged.

Sometimes she came back a bit disoriented, but always, always she was so happy to see us.

"Oh, it's you!" she would exclaim. "I love you so much," and then she would go only to return again, surprised and delighted to see us once again. "Oh, it's you, I love you so much!" Each return was new. She was new and so were we.

At one point she became very lucid for a longer stretch of time. Taking Shya's hand, she gave him the equivalent of a dying sage's blessing.

"You know, I must admit, Shya, that when you were younger, I never thought you would turn out, but you did. I am very proud of you."

Wow, what a gift! We all cried as Shya and she held hands. Then she drifted away. Upon her return, Ida looked him in the eye and said, "You are going to be very famous someday," before she left again.

Ida was in a rhythm of her own now. She didn't need us to keep her alive. Her body closed itself down bit by bit. Her race was almost run.

Two nights later, she finally slipped away for good.

Ida was laid to rest in a beautiful mahogany casket that Rhoda, Shya's sister, had picked out. Before the service, the family met.

It was a sad day. But it was also a day where we shared stories about Ida Speiler who got married and became Ida Kane. These stories are a legacy we preserved to hand down to our children.

To get the ball rolling, Ida's only remaining sibling told a little about Ida's early life. Ruth, a tiny, almost-replica of her sister, stood and recited some facts of old that were new to us.

"Ida was born on Rivington Street near Delancey," she began. These streets are on Manhattan's Lower East Side.

"Things were pretty normal at first, and then the Depression came. My father lost his job. Everyone was out of work, and Ida got a job and supported the whole family. She was thirteen then."

I felt a rush as if someone had poured ice water over my head. The hairs rose on my arms. Of course. Now this puzzle was completed. I imagined a petite child of thirteen, laboring to feed her siblings and both parents. She had to support Harry, Eddy, Ruth, Matt, her mother, her father, and herself, seven in all.

"You have no idea what it is like to be dependent on money and then lose it," she had said. "I swore I would never become dependent on money again!"

Later, during the service, I gave my own silent prayer: *Oh, Ida, Ida. I understand. I am so, so sorry. Things must have hurt really badly. I realize now that when you were a child and desperately fighting to help your parents and all of your brothers and sister survive, you swore you would conserve money, no matter what. You could not possibly have known how that promise would prevent you from getting help for your daughter Sandra. You have had to carry such a burden of guilt. I feel such compassion for you. I love you so much. I understand. You are forgiven, Ida. I hope now you can finally rest in peace.*

Ida was a beautiful, caring person whose actions had become twisted by the traumas to her heart. The decisions she had made dictated her life and caused her and those around her great pain. But given the logic system that evolved from her life circumstances, that was the only appropriate response she could see.

Our not judging her actions and holding them as "bad" allowed the resulting pain she felt to dissolve so that she could finally know peace, and so could we.

A while back, the two of us saw an episode of the television show "Justice Files." One segment of the program portrayed the sentencing of a man convicted of the brutal rape and murder of a beautiful young girl. As part of the proceedings, members of the slain girl's family were allowed to stand up and address the defendant and judge so as to foster healing and closure for the bereaved. The girl's mother stood before the man who had just been sentenced to life in prison for killing her daughter and forgave him. The mother stated that she couldn't find it in her heart to hate him, because if she did that hatred would eat away at her heart. She forgave him and hoped that God would watch over him, wherever he went from there.

The person who is really freed when you forgive someone is you. Most people have no idea that you hold their actions as transgressions, so the person mainly punished when you hold a grudge is you. Again, even if you are "correct," if you are being right about how another is wrong, something alive in you dies.

6

THE BIRTH OF THE PRESENT

*O*nce you begin to forgive people and events from your past and let go of your history, the present starts to emerge. The approach or paradigm we are suggesting does not involve fixing your past or fixing your problems. This is confusing to most people because they naturally want to do something to make things better. They want a fix-it technique because they have the idea "the more you do, the more results you produce."

There is another paradigm called "being."

If you are being in this moment, all problems disappear automatically because problems are past/future oriented. All problems are a projection toward the future of possible realities based on your past.

If you let go of the past and you let go of the future, there are no more problems. And it may sound glib to say this, but it really is true: the more willing you are to be here and let go of your history and your story, the more life can unfold in this moment.

HOW SWEET IT IS

There is an old story about a man walking through the jungle. Sensing a presence, the man looked over his shoulder and saw a tiger slinking through the foliage, following him. Quickening his pace, the fellow followed the path he was on until he reached a cliff. Looking back once again, he saw the tiger was still there and coming closer. Standing with his toes over the edge, the man noticed that there was a vine running down the cliff face, and he swung out onto the vine in order to escape the tiger. Just as he quickly lowered himself down, the tiger jumped. Slashing over the edge with her paw, the tiger narrowly missed catching the man as he made his descent. As the man started to work his way down the cliff face, he looked down to the bottom and saw yet another tiger, the mate of the one at the top. The tigers settled down to wait. Hanging there, the man saw that two mice, a white one and a black one, had started gnawing on the vine above his head. It was only a matter of time before the vine gave way. Looking off to one side, he noticed a wild strawberry gleaming crimson in the sunlight. He picked it, put it in his mouth, and tasted . . . how sweet it was!

Worrying about the future and missing the sweetness of the moment seems to be a way of life for most people. Of course, there are plenty of things to worry about today, if that is what you are used to. There was plenty to worry about in our parents' day also, and in our grandparents', and so on back through time. And yet they survived. We are all a living testament to that. Perhaps we worry as a part of the culture we were raised in, as a survival strategy passed down from generation to generation. Have you ever stopped to think that worry is not an integral part of well-being but something extra, unneeded, and unexamined that we have absorbed from those around us?

You can taste the wild strawberries that exist around you in your everyday life by being here in this moment rather than worrying about things you cannot immediately do anything about, such as the state of the world, global warming, political conflict, wars, etc. Those things do exist, but in this moment so does the chair you are sitting in, the air you are breathing, and the floor under your feet.

Perhaps you tend to worry about something more personal, such as your finances, the state of your relationship, or your health. Well, does worrying actually accomplish anything positive? Worry is the mind's projection of possible futures, based on what we have experienced or known from the past.

Being here in this moment is the great transformational agent. If you are actually engaged in being here, then life does not have to repeat itself. Previously unknown, unseen creative solutions can present themselves. If you are here, you are available to see them.

There is a country western song Tim McGraw sings about a man who discovers he has a potentially terminal disease and goes out and does all the things he only dreamed of doing . . . and many he hadn't even considered—riding a bull, going fishing, being a true friend, talking more kindly, allowing himself to love deeply and be forgiving.

For the most part, we don't live our lives as though it is our last day. We do things that if we were dying we would never indulge in. If the end were near, we wouldn't waste those few precious moments. The trick is in discovering how to maintain this sense of urgency and vitality without threatening ourselves with dire circumstances such as imminent death. Although the song "Live Like You Were Dying" is just a song, it represents what can happen if you engage in your life without preference, without listening to the story of whether or not you feel like doing something, and without thinking that this moment doesn't matter.

How do you engage in your life as if this moment matters when you are truly out of touch with that experience and are lost in a loop of worry, you might ask? Well, you could start by washing your dishes, making your bed, cleaning up your office, completing those things that you have left incomplete and that you ignore by worrying about other things. What if worry were just a sophisticated way to procrastinate? Have you ever considered that if you are really busy, fully engaged, getting things done, you rarely have time or interest in complaining about your life?

So if you need a place to start, look around you. Handling any little incompletion is a great start. Then move on to the next thing. You might start with the things you like to do first. Get into a rhythm. Then keep including what's next. You will be pleasantly surprised how, as you handle the minutia of your life, the answers to how to handle the "big" things magically appear.

THE PHILOSOPHER'S STONE

If you can stop blaming how you have turned out on your past, your life will magically transform. Forward and back, forever. Just by getting here now. As mentioned in the chapter on Instantaneous Transformation, the philosopher's stone was something from ancient alchemy, the forerunner of chemistry, that was purported to transmute base metals such as lead into gold.

That is what is possible for everyone. It requires only one thing—getting into the moment. It does not require thinking about the moment, nor trying to change or fix any aspect of yourself.

There is no work involved in Instantaneous Transformation. Transformation, as we said, is a state of being. It is a way to be in your life, and it isn't something that you do, like a practice. You can't *do* being transformed. You can be transformed.

> There is a modern-day philosopher's stone—being in this moment. And what it does is transform ordinary, mundane lives into exquisite, magnificent lives.

When you are living in the moment, there is nothing you need to achieve, fix, or get rid of, and a deep sense of satisfaction radiates from within rather than being just out of reach. When you are in the moment, what was once held as base becomes golden.

THE PARADOX OF BEING AND DOING

Enlightenment is a state of being and cannot be achieved through doing. Yet all of us are trained to do things to accomplish the ends we desire. For instance, you might ask, "How can I quiet my mind? What meditation can I do to achieve a state of well-being? Tell me what to do and I will do that."

The paradox is that there is nothing to do to achieve a state of well-being. There are things that can be done and still there is nothing to do. So how do we approach this paradox, this apparent conundrum, and actually discover how to live our lives directly, in each moment, authentically, not as a contrivance of doing?

There is a delicate balance between engaging in an act, in the accomplishment of a task, and the presence one brings that is not based in trying to get the task over with. This is not an easy thing to talk about. It is as though we are trying to describe your favorite ice cream so that you can actually taste it.

It has been our experience that when a person is present, he or she frequently comes up with profound solutions to what were problematic events and irreconcilable mysteries while taking a shower or doing the dishes, while sleeping or resting. The answer comes from someplace other than the logic system of rational thought.

We are all trained to *do*. We have been taught in school how to accomplish things by doing. If there is a problem, we think, "What do I do to change or fix the problem, and how can I accomplish that as quickly as possible?"

There is another possibility, the possibility of being with the situation and noticing the urge to make a resolution. Being with the situation, rather than trying to do something to change or fix it, can resolve it.

You have to be present to the action in which you are involved, without trying to get it over with but doing it for the pure experience of the action itself. The paradox is that you want to accomplish the task. And it is not about accomplishing the task; it is about being there for it.

When you experience something, it completes itself. Anything left over is a "nonexperience," something that has been resisted so it sticks around and adds baggage to your life. You can either surrender to the demands your life puts on you, in which case you are not resisting the experience and it completes itself, adding energy back to your life, or you can succumb to having to do what your life requests of you, in which case you will complain or resent that you have to do it and it will take energy from you and cause you pain.

For example, one evening our friend Bob had a heart attack. This near-death experience was obviously not something he would have preferred. On that night, Bob experienced severe heartburn and strange, debilitating sensations in his chest. His wife called 911, an EMS unit quickly arrived, and he was rushed to the hospital. When he got there, it was apparent from the doctor's demeanor that he was in serious condition. And in fact he was.

The heart attack was severe enough that Bob had to be placed on a respirator, an apparatus that breathes for you. Here is what Bob had to say about this traumatic event:

"I don't know how it happened, but there was a calmness in me and a detachment from the panic that was going on around me. I was simply the observer of the experience and I was just being there. I was placed on the respirator, and eventually an interesting thing happened. As I got 'better' and regained my health I found that my desire to be in control and to do something about the situation returned.

A respirator in effect breathes for you. It pumps air in and takes air out. What happened was that I wanted to control the rate of my breathing on my own. When this happened, I was fighting against the moment, and it was extremely distressing. Of course I wanted to get better, but it was important to realize that in that moment there was nothing to do to accomplish this and that, in fact, doing something was getting in the way.

"Since that time, my wife and I have implemented a healthier lifestyle with diet, nutrition, and exercise, and yet I find that doing these things without bringing my presence to it is not satisfying. However, when I go about my life with excellence and presence as if it is my idea to be fit, not as a reaction to having been ill, I find that my life is extremely rich, rewarding, and satisfying."

Bob's brush with death left him with an interesting perspective about life. He realized that he could either resist the way his life was showing up and drag his feet through the things he had to do (this could be termed *succumbing*), or he could surrender to these demands and do them as though they were his choice in the first place. Bob realized that he could bring his presence and awareness to what he was involved in and fully engage in these things, which led to satisfaction, well-being, and a sense of control in his own life.

The experience of the respirator was the first in a series of surrendering to being "out of control," which has subsequently led him into the experience of ultimate control. We spent time with Bob during the months after his heart attack and got to watch him reformat his lifestyle. There were times when he felt victimized by his circumstances and *succumbed* to eating in a healthier manner (no binging on french fries or French toast and butter), and during this time he felt deprived. As he learned to *surrender* to the dietary shift and to eat the foods on his heart-healthy list as if it were his choice, not something imposed on him, he regained his relish for eating, only now his food consumption didn't have negative consequences.

HAPPINESS

From the time we were children, we have absorbed the idea that it is better to be happy than unhappy. Everyone knows it is better to be happy and joyous than sad or angry or upset or unsure of what to do with one's life. So people try to be happy.

In the United States we pursue "the American Dream." We have been taught that landing the right job or acquiring certain possessions will bring us satisfaction. And of course many believe that finding that perfect someone, our soul mate, will bring eternal bliss. Obviously this isn't true. How many of us have found the relationship of our dreams only to have it turn into a nightmare?

Remember how excited you were when you got that doll or toy or your favorite hero on a baseball card? And later how it felt to finally get your first car or stereo system or that engagement ring? Today those toys and possessions are long since discarded, forgotten, or taken for granted in your day-to-day life. Especially those of us who have been very

good at acquiring things have discovered that this form of happiness is transitory at best.

Some have found their "soul mate" only to keep wondering why other areas of their lives aren't working and wondering if maybe there is more to life than just a great relationship. It wasn't too long ago that having a family was going to do it—there was the assumption that having a child would infuse one's relationship and life with purpose and meaning. And yet these days the cat is out of the bag—raising a child is not always a panacea; it can be hard work and stressful at times too.

So what are we to do? It seems as if our myths and superstitions, which were purported to be the signposts for utopia, are being discarded along the road. Yet most of us are left with the same question, which sings to us, repeating like variations on a theme throughout our lives: How can I achieve true and lasting happiness in this lifetime?

How to Find Happiness

The two of us, after much searching and working on ourselves, pushing and prodding, stumbled into something that has led to an ongoing sense of satisfaction and well-being—a state that includes happiness as well as the entire range of human emotions. We have found This Moment and in so doing have found the answer to that age-old quest for lasting fulfillment and satisfaction. True and lasting happiness can only be found now, in this moment.

Part of the reason most people's lives are not happy is that they have designated "happy" as a desired state and then they resist or judge those states that are not. This locks them into the emotion or condition that they are resisting (the First Principle of Instantaneous Transformation).

Until you are willing to be the way you are in any given moment, you can never be truly happy, because happiness is only one of many emotions that human beings are capable of experiencing.

If we resist whatever emotion happens to be there in this moment in favor of a preferred one, for example, happiness, we are stuck with the emotion we are resisting. How many times have you seen somebody pretending to be happy when actually he or she is in pain? Smiling over the pain, pretending that it doesn't exist, is a form of resistance. As a result, the pain, sadness, or anger will not only stick around but grow stronger.

What we are saying is being willing to experience what is happening in your life in this moment will allow for completion. For instance, if you are experiencing sadness and you don't resist it and you don't try to get rid of it and you don't try to be happy instead, but just let yourself feel the emotion, it will complete itself.

This is a perfect example of the Three Principles of Instantaneous Transformation. If you resist an emotion, that causes it to stay in place—this is the First Principle. Next, you can't truly experience being happy when you are in truth already sad—this is the Second Principle. And anything you allow to be exactly as it is, without trying to fix it, or change it, or pretend that it is different, better, or even worse than it is, will complete itself and cease to dominate your life—this is the Third Principle. Judging an emotion as if it is bad or the wrong one to be having keeps it in place. But awareness, simple nonjudgmental seeing or experiencing, allows even the strongest of emotions to complete themselves.

Most people avoid experiences or emotions they consider negative. When these "negative" experiences or emotions are avoided and we try to live our lives pretending they don't exist, they persist, and no amount of achievement or acquiring or cosmetic surgery will change them. So we become prisoners of our attempt to avoid unpleasant things in our lives in favor of "happiness."

The essence of true happiness comes out of your willingness to experience what is between you and happiness.

Most people are not willing to have the emotions, thoughts, and feelings they are having, and instead resist them, so they have to settle for a pale facsimile of what true happiness is. But you can't be with sadness in order to get over it, for that is not being with it at all. This is actually just the First Principle in disguise. When you are being with something with the agenda to rid yourself of it, this is actually resisting what is. It is just an attempt to manipulate yourself so that you can once again achieve what your mind says is going to make you happy.

Have you ever been with a person who is truly sad? We are not talking about wallowing around, feeling sorry for him- or herself or dramatizing the emotion so that he or she doesn't have to feel, but someone who is actually allowing him- or herself to touch into a deep well of sadness or grief, perhaps over the passing of a loved one. Or perhaps you have been with someone close to death. Being with someone in this state is rich. It is alive. It can be healing, and, surprisingly, it can feel wonderful too. Sometimes in these moments people discover how to truly be intimate—they rediscover their ability to love and have compassion.

> Only by being the way you are can you find that elusive state of contentment.

7

WORMS: WRITE ONCE READ MANY

The decisions that we made early in our lives often remain unchallenged and forgotten. Have you considered that your internal dialogue may actually be a collection of ancient recordings that have no real relevance to this moment?

It has been said that we have approximately 187,000 thoughts a day, 98 percent of which we had the day before and the day before that. People's minds operate like a tape recorder on playback, feeding us old information as if it were brand-new.

The commentary about your life that plays inside the privacy of your own thoughts is like a bright penny hung on a string. Sometimes the string rotates one way and the light of the day catches your penny and you think to yourself that you are doing pretty good. Other times your thoughts twist the other direction, illuminating the idea that what you are doing is no good at all or that nothing you do will ever really make a difference. Most of us are mesmerized by that twisting and turning penny. We love it when it gyrates in the direction that praises our strengths and bemoan the times when it swings back to those old self-deprecating thoughts.

If you want to live in a truly satisfying manner, it is essential to take your attention off the lure of that bright penny, off your compelling internal commentary whether it be for or against your current circumstances.

Your mind operates like a computer. In computer technology there is an acronym for a type of data storage called a WORM, which stands for Write Once Read Many. It is a system for permanently keeping information. The data is indelibly written and can never be altered. It is then available to be read as many times as you want as though new.

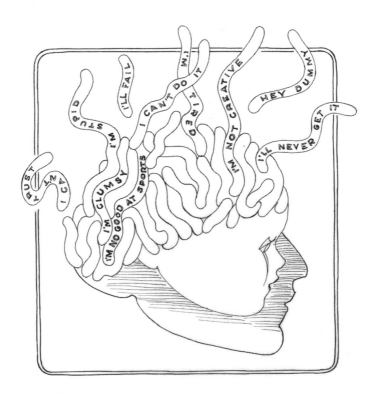

Our minds too are full of WORMs. In moments of stress or contraction, or times when our survival seems threatened, we make decisions to avoid repeating those things that we think caused the crisis. Decisions, even those made long ago, are stored in your mind in such a way that you can read them many times as though brand-new, true in this moment, applicable to your current circumstances.

Once these decisions are written (stated to ourselves), we hold them as truth over time in our minds. Then, when a current situation in our environment feels similar to a time when we made that decision, our mind accesses the WORM and it plays back as if it were totally new information.

Here's an example of how it works. Let's say little Billy was called upon to answer a question at school. He thought he had the right answer, but when he said it out loud it was wrong. The other kids laughed, and in Billy's mind, even the teacher seemed to be making fun of him. Billy then hunched his shoulders, slid lower in his seat, and said to himself . . .

This is the genesis of a WORM. In this case it happened when Billy didn't like how he felt and wanted to avoid feeling the discomfort again. The logic system is something like: "Yuck, I didn't like that. I don't want that to happen again. Maybe it is better to say I don't know, even if I do. Then I won't have to risk being laughed at and humiliated again." So Billy sets in place the beginning of a life strategy, but he forgets he made that decision. Then, as an adult, Bill wonders why he is so tentative in business meetings. He is frustrated that ideas and answers always seem to be on the tip of his

Here are some sample WORMs. Are any of yours in here?

- I will never let that happen again.
- I'll never be like them.
- I won't let myself be vulnerable again.
- I can't trust men.
- I can't trust women.
- I'll never be successful, why try?
- I am not attractive.
- I'm done with dating.
- I'm not creative.
- I'm no good at sports.
- I'm not intellectual enough.
- I'm stupid.
- I'm tired.
- I can't do it.
- Money is hard to come by.
- No matter what I do it's not good enough.
- I'm clumsy.
- I'm no good with my hands.
- They don't like me because I am too . . . small, fat, skinny, old, young, poor, rich, short, tall, uneducated, overqualified, nice, mean, etc.

There are, conservatively speaking, a million other WORMs, but for the sake of brevity we will leave the list short.

tongue but others always seem to be faster at expressing them and they get the credit, not he.

Sometimes WORMs are not only thought processes but also emotions. Take the person who used to cry as a child when caught doing something "bad." Because she was already upset, her parent didn't have the heart to administer punishment. Thus the child learns to survive via tears. Now, as an adult, whenever things get pressured or mistakes are made at work, tears spring unbidden to her eyes. Write Once Read Many. As an adult, you may not appreciate some of these reflexive, mechanical behaviors, but these ways of being and relating worked for us when we were younger. They were recorded, and now the mind replays them as strategic moves and our lives are an endless repetition of the past.

When there is a lapse in activity, or when under stress, your mind will go to a familiar conversation by default much in the same way a computer has a screen saver that fills your monitor with messages or images of flying toasters. Perhaps the "I'm still hungry" or "I can't handle this, I'm out of here!" message is no more current or serious than a toaster with wings except that you forgot you were listening to an old recording.

It is easy to be fooled, though. At least with a phonograph, we can hear the telltale scratchy sounds of old-time recording techniques. However, with your own personal, mental WORMs, they get more sophisticated and polished as you do, kind of an automatic courtesy upgrade.

Here is a personal example of just such a WORM as told from Shya's point of view.

THE MAKING OF A WORM

When I was eight years old, I spent several long bored afternoons at my father's dress factory in New York's garment district. I made long circuits around the large cutting tables, trailing a finger and looking for things with which to occupy myself. The cutter at this time was William Salereno. He would cut the material to be sewn into fine dresses. William had a magical drawer under the cutting tables filled with oddments—pipe cleaners, paper clips, an old stamp, a penny or two. He also had boxes and boxes of toothpicks. Oh, how I wanted some. I dreamed of all the things I could make with those tiny slivers of wood—houses and trains and racing cars. I begged and cajoled and finally William let me have one precious box. I set to work with a bottle of glue and high hopes of creating the car that was in my mind's eye. Several long frustrating hours later, my dream car turned out as a dismal failure, lumpy and misshapen, nothing like my intent.

And there it was, the beginning of my own personal WORM: I was clumsy, no good with my hands, unable to build anything of worth. Utterly defeated, I threw it all away and sat with my legs kicking the rungs of my chair, waiting for the long, long afternoon to end.

Today I still have this story. According to the WORM I am still clumsy, no good with my hands, unskilled, a failure, and unable to build anything of value. And yet, in my twenties I worked as a cabinetmaker, and later I built my own home from logs I felled myself. In my dining room currently sits a smooth old black walnut harvest table, with wood I lovingly hand-milled and smoothed and shaped, although I left the edges "live" with the bark still intact. The grain is fine and so is the workmanship. It will likely be just as beautiful long after my grandchildren are grown. I am "no good" at tying fishing flies either, according to this story. And yet not only am I passionate about tying them, but Ariel has caught all of her world-record fish on my flies. And yes, in these "clumsy, good for nothing" hands she has found pleasure for more than twenty-five years.

Yes, I have my story and then there is the obvious. We have all told ourselves big and little untruths since we were children. Luckily, our stories are but gossamer. Awareness, simply seeing them without judging what we see, is the gentle breeze that floats them away.

DECISIONS

If physicists are accurate, then the universe is always expanding. Therefore, if you make a rule to live by based on WORMs such as "I will never date again" or "I will never depend on money again," then it has to be limiting even if the basic premise was sound. Your universe will keep expanding, but you will keep your life confined to the arbitrary, narrow limit you set upon it as a child. Simply by living out of a rule or decision from the past, you are destined to be an inhibited, fettered version of yourself.

It is akin to buying a little potted sapling and taking it out to the forest where the ground is fertile, where it will get just the right amount of sunshine, rain, and wind. But when you plant the tree you leave it in its original pot and plant it container and all. The pot then defines how far the tree can grow—not the lush, verdant forest around it. It acts as a boundary that determines how deep the roots can reach and therefore how high its limbs can climb. The pot, our deci-

sions, effectively stunt our ability to grow, and we become root-bound, stagnant in our lives.

It is important to differentiate between deciding and choosing. Please don't get caught up in the words being used here. It is not our intention to get the readers of this book to manipulate their language in order to speak in a new and improved system where using the word *choice* is better than *decision*. Rather, see if you can catch the distinction between the two so you become empowered in your life. It may be a bit confusing at first and seem to be primarily an exercise in semantics. However, the difference between the essence of decision and choice may hold the key to your discovery of Instantaneous Transformation and true fulfillment.

8

DECISIONS VERSUS CHOICES

*L*et us look at the differences between deciding and choosing. A decision is intellectually determined and is made primarily through a logical thought process. A choice, on the other hand, is a selection made after consideration that is reflective of your heartfelt desires or authentic wishes. In other words, when you decide something, you weigh the pros and cons, basically making two columns where you add up the arguments for and against an action. Depending on which has more weight, you follow the prescribed course.

A choice, however, takes all of those pros and cons into account. But once you examine all of the information, it allows for intuitive leaps, heartfelt moves, and creative alternatives that might not have been suggested by mere factual analysis and simple deductive reasoning. Decisions are reasonable. Choices, while including logic, are not based solely in reasons.

DECISIONS

At their very best, decisions we make and follow were made by a younger, less sophisticated version of ourselves. Would you seriously ask a two- or

Choices are the expression of your heart. A decision is the mandate of a WORM.

three-year-old what you should do with your life, set that decision in stone, and then live out the rest of your life based on that advice? Yet this is essentially what many of us have done. We live out of the decisions our minds reached when we were very young.

It is kind of like a squirrel that gets caught in the middle of the road in the path of an onrushing vehicle. It doesn't know which direction to go for safety, and in its terror it scurries back and forth, helter-skelter, in jerky little movements and a rush of adrenaline. Luckily, the car or truck happens to miss crushing the squirrel. But now it has filed this behavior as a survival strategy. It was coincidental that the squirrel didn't get flattened. Its life was saved in spite of its remaining in the roadway. Our minds work in the same manner. They record all of the data, even the coincidental information, sometimes linking the two. Usually we don't realize that we achieve goals or move forward in our lives in spite of the self-deprecating thought patterns and self-reproaches that we mistakenly linked as an integral part of our survival.

"Are all decisions made in a moment of contraction?" you might ask. The answer is yes. Let's say you do something that is "right" and you get rewarded or recognized. While basking in the good feelings, you say, "Wow, this really worked. I am going to keep doing that!" But this decision is based in the idea that you can't trust yourself in the future to make the right choices that will produce the good feelings again. The mind wants to systematize what it thinks you did right as well as what it thinks you did wrong in order to ensure your survival. And perhaps a good portion of the time this survival strategy may be sound. But sooner or later doing anything by rote will get you into trouble. Repeating even "good" moves gets tedious because it cuts out the possibility of new, creative solutions and locks us into an old way of life.

So how does one recognize when a seemingly current choice is just an old WORM? There are some telltale signs that will help you recognize when you are authentically expressing yourself as opposed to when you are stuck in the groove of an old but perhaps not so favorite song.

Oddly enough, sometimes what you decide to do and what you would choose to do may be the same. There is, however, a vast contrast in the experience of satisfaction depending on the route you take to your final destination.

You can really see the difference in two individuals' approaches to goals. One has decided that the life she has now is not good enough and she is going to get a new job or relationship or buy something to fix the problem. This is a problem/solution framework rooted in change that does not lead to the satisfaction that comes with Instantaneous Transformation and living in this current moment of now. When this person reaches a goal, she may feel a momentary sense of victory, but dissatisfaction is still lurking just around the corner. Then come the what-ifs and self-doubts and the pattern starts all over again once the pressure of life builds.

The other individual may have the same goals as the first. But even if he takes similar actions, if he is not coming from a context that something is wrong or deficient with him, then each step of the journey can be fulfilling and exciting in and of itself. When this second individual reaches a goal, it is simply an extension of the profound satisfaction that he is already experiencing in life.

Another indicator of being in the grips of a WORM is something that could be called the déjà-vu factor. This is the feeling you get when you are poised to say the thing that you know will get you into a fight but can't seem to help doing it. Or it is when you are upset at something or someone in your current environment, but it is the same old feeling that you have had many, many times before.

If you are making a life move and are defensive about it, you can be sure there is a decision in there somewhere. A choice is not defendable. How can you adequately explain or prove intuitive hunches or knowing something in your heart?

So how do we get rid of the WORMs we have made? Here is the good news and the bad news: we can't. Don't forget what WORM stands for: Write Once Read Many. These decisions are set in place and available to be read forever.

However, you can bypass them, and awareness is the key. If you notice your behavior, like a modern-day anthropologist, it will allow you to disengage from old decisions. What it takes is neutral observation without punishing, chastising, or even congratulating yourself for what you see.

If you observe your thoughts without judging what you see, it is enough to dissolve the mechanical nature of your life.

In conclusion, you basically have two options: to operate through old decisions or to look freshly at your life and see what you want to do from your heart and your truth rather than from an old agenda. Don't worry if you have made decisions or choices in the past. Everyone has done his or her share of both. Second-guessing yourself can easily lead to the creation of a whole new set of decisions.

In fact, after reading this chapter, you could decide to not make decisions any more—you are only going to make choices because choices are better. Ahh, the mind is tricky.

GREENER PASTURES

Once we saw a goat put out to graze in a lush field. The grass was high and feeding was plentiful. But the goat wasn't satisfied. It made a funny picture as it strained toward the field next door. Its front legs were suspended midair, dangling over the fence as it vainly reached for a tempting bit of green just out of reach. Of course the grass wasn't any richer or higher or more succulent in the next pasture, but try telling that to the goat.

What pastures are you straining after? Most people are strenuously reaching toward what they think will make them happy or satisfied, straining toward something more, better, or different. The problem with this is that there is always something else that needs to be bought or produced in order for you to be happy or satisfied. Truthfully, in this moment, you can only have what you have. Anything you yearn for robs you of the possibility of reveling in the richness of your life.

People get so driven by where they are going that they miss their lives. You may actually be rushing ahead to finish this book, trying to answer some question or fulfill some agenda. While you are trying so hard to get something from the writing, you are not actually there for the reading.

Many of us live our lives as if we are looking through a telephoto lens on a camera. A telephoto lens focuses in on an object in the distance and excludes everything peripheral to that object. So you miss everything happening around you. Instantaneous Transformation is more like a wide-angle lens. It holds everything in focus whether it is close up or far away, and there is three-dimensionality and depth to what you see. The telephoto lens, on the other hand, makes things much more two-dimensional or flat; you lose the depth of field. When people are lost in a change modality, they feel annoyed when things "intrude" and interrupt their flow toward where they are headed. In a transformational approach, life becomes a dance of noticing what is rather than a tense experience of trying to exclude everything that does not seem on track to producing the things we think we want in the future to make us happy or fulfilled.

It could be said that life is an unfolding, moment to moment, and we have preferences that frequently disagree with how life unfolds, because we are trying to get somewhere rather than be where we are. We think something better is going to come along because this isn't it, when in fact this moment is all there is. This moment IS it.

People are so busy worrying about what they don't have or how it is going to turn out in the future, they rarely allow themselves to really relish and enjoy the way things are right now. Life becomes a worry about what isn't, rather than a celebration of what is. For if we, like the goat, invest our energy only in wanting what we don't have and lusting after tantalizing goals currently out of reach, satisfaction is set aside for a mythical someday that never comes.

THE ATTAINMENT OF GOALS AND SATISFACTION

Folks are waiting to be saved from their current state or circumstances by a blinding flash of insight, or perhaps on a less esoteric level by winning the lottery. They want to graduate to their idea of what it means to have arrived, to have achieved success, and to truly be an adult. In spiritual vernacular this means we feel we should have become "enlightened" by now, and nothing should cause us to fall off center, be upset, or become ill ever again. Truthfully, though, satisfaction is not circumstantially determined.

People believe falsely that if only they had perfect health or the right job, the right boyfriend or girlfriend, the right toys to play with, then they would be satisfied. Yet there are doctors who find doctoring boring and frustrating. There are teachers who are just waiting to retire. There are people who have everything money can buy, but all their gadgets and gizmos give them no pleasure. Others are certain they have found that special someone, yet even another's love can't fill the void.

If you are satisfied, you bring your satisfaction to the moment and fill the circumstances of your life with that sat-

Most of us live in a con- | isfaction. If you are dissatisfied, how-
stant state of complaint. | ever, no one and nothing can produce
contentment for you. If you listen to
your internal commentary regarding
your likes and dislikes, it will prevent you from experiencing
a satisfied life. In *Hsin-hsin Ming*, written fourteen hundred
years ago by the third Zen patriarch, Seng-ts'an, it says, "To
set up what you like against what you dislike is the disease
of the mind."

Whenever you compare your current circumstances to
how you would prefer your life to look, the result is always
the same: dissatisfaction. People haven't realized that what
is going on in their life in any given moment of now really,
truly is the only way their life could appear. We may have
preferences, but it is rare that our preferences are congruent
with our current experience. In other words, if you are comparing how it currently is to how you would prefer it to be,
you rob yourself of any possibility of satisfaction. It is kind
of like wishing your Volkswagen would sprout wings and fly
you to Europe for a vacation. That is not the design function
of an automobile. And wishing won't make it so.

How often do we leave tasks undone simply because we
do not like to do them, but then these incompletions plague
us throughout our days? How often is our sleep disturbed
by thoughts of incomplete projects or events that happened
that weren't to our liking?

Our internal conversation or dialogue, the voice we
listen to that we attach our name to and believe to be us,
is constantly complaining and nattering about how what is

going on in our lives is wrong—how it should be different or better than it is. This habituated way of interacting with our lives has been passed down to us from generation to generation. As infants, the way we learned was to absorb the culture that we found ourselves in. This is why everybody who was raised in the South has a southern accent and everyone who was raised in New England sounds like a Yankee.

Spirituality exists in all aspects of our lives when we experience life directly, not through the filter of our enculturation, judgments, agendas, or thought processes. You can only do one thing at a time. You can either think about what is happening in your life or you can be in the experience of what is happening in your life, moment to moment. This does not mean that we stop thinking. It does, however, mean that the voice that judges, evaluates, and rates how you are doing fades into the background and no longer dominates your life.

Why we say that working on yourself doesn't work is that the process never ends. If you are working on yourself, then your starting premise is that there is something wrong with you that needs to be fixed and you can never fix yourself enough to feel good about yourself. There will always be something else to compare yourself with and you will always fall short. If, however, you discover how to be satisfied the way you are, you will have an excellent life. And, contrary to popular belief, if you are satisfied with who you are, you will be empowered to expand rather than become complacent.

When you discover how to access and live in the present moment, satisfaction and well-being are the result. It is about redirecting your attention away from yourself as a problem and getting engaged in the requests that life makes upon you, discovering how to say yes to what is happening now, in your life, in this moment. This is Instantaneous Transformation.

Enlightenment, satisfaction, waking up happens when you interact with your life as though you are doing exactly what you are supposed to be doing and your circumstances are exactly what they are supposed to be rather than complaining about your life. This state of enlightenment is not elusive. What it requires is your getting here and now. It is simple, deceptively simple, so simple that it can be difficult to understand.

It is possible for you right now, given your current circumstance, to discover your state of being as enlightened. In fact, the only way to realize enlightenment is to have the current circumstances that you have in your life in this moment.

ENGAGING IN THE MOMENT

So how does one live life directly? How does one become satisfied? Well, here is a hint. Engaging in any activity as fully as you know how is the beginning. If you are washing the dishes and find that you are talking to yourself in your mind about whether or not you want to be doing what you are doing, this is a clue that you are not fully engaged.

Here is the tricky part: If you are preoccupied or complaining, that is all you can be doing in that moment (Second Principle of Instantaneous Transformation). *That is* your moment. However, with awareness (nonjudgmental seeing of what is—Third Principle), the conversation you are listening to will complete itself or you will be able to intentionally disengage from it and redirect your energy.

One of the side benefits of living life in the moment is that relatively mundane acts take on a sense of fullness. Your actions become appropriate, not based on past decisions or agendas. Agendas are those ideas we have about what will fulfill us or produce satisfaction in the future. These agendas all come from the known. They come from what society holds to be true (or resistance to society) rather than from your experience of what is actually fulfilling for you. Therefore, fulfillment or satisfaction can never be achieved by completing these agendas unless you are already satisfied. True satisfaction comes from living your life directly, not judging yourself for how you are doing.

Living life directly includes your agendas and goals but is not merely driving forward to achieve them. For example, you may have the goal to be physically fit and plan a regimen at the gym to support this desire. People who exercise with the intention of experiencing purity of motion and having optimum form while performing each move will come away enlivened from the experience. They will also be simultaneously moving forward toward being physically fit. However, people who look in the mirror and complain about what they see, those who exercise in order to be all right someday, inadvertently reinforce the known story that

Resistance to the circumstances of your life perpetuates dissatisfaction and generates pain.

something is wrong with them, and even when they achieve their goal, their sense of being wrong lingers.

Accepting, allowing, and interacting with your life as though it is exactly as it should be, without making yourself wrong (or right) for what you discover, is the way to Self-Realization. The path to enlightenment is to reveal to yourself, honestly, the ways in which you are mechanically interacting with your life—without trying to do something about it or change it. "What!" you might say. "Don't change it?" Yes, Self-Realization lies in awareness and not in a problem/solution framework.

Awareness, as we have said, is a state of being, not doing. If you become aware of a behavior pattern, the simple awareness of that pattern, allowing yourself to be in that pattern, and allowing that pattern to complete itself is enough to transform it (Third Principle of Instantaneous Transformation). If you do something to change the pattern, it will perpetuate it (First Principle).

We are not suggesting that there aren't things that must be done in our daily lives. Awareness can—and in many instances, must—include doing. This concept is illustrated in a story about a master and his disciple who were traveling through the desert. One evening they came to an oasis where they bedded down for the night. When they awoke in the morning, their camels were gone. Since tethering the camels each night was the disciple's responsibility, the master asked him whether he had secured them for the night. The disciple replied, "No, master. You teach that we should trust in Allah. I was trusting that Allah would take care of the camels for us." To this his master responded, "Yes, trust in Allah, but you must also tether the camels."

When you are aware, you act appropriately, doing what is needed and wanted. These actions aren't born of a decision to do it right. They won't be reflective of your agenda to "do better next time." Your actions, the things you do, become authentic expressions of your True Self rather than the execution of something you have decided to do in an attempt to be a "better" you. To decide (same root as suicide and homicide) is similar to being "dead right"; both kill off the alternatives.

Awareness results in erasure or completion because awareness is nonjudgmental and without preference. Sengts'an, the author of *Hsin-hsin Ming*, also said that "the Great Way is not difficult for those who have no preferences." It is those same preferences that come into play when things don't go the way you think they should. If you invest in being right about what you prefer, then you generate pain and dissatisfaction and all creativity comes to a halt. Simply notice that things are different from what you would prefer and the way opens again. And again, acceptance does not lead to complacency. Rather it empowers the individual to become responsive rather than reactive, to make real choices about life based on what is really taking place versus decisions based on old successes and failures. While it is true that this day and age bring challenges and changes that our ancestors never had to consider, it is also true that some ideas can stand the test of time.

> The Great Way is not difficult for those who have no preferences. When love and hate are both absent everything becomes clear and undisguised. Make the smallest distinction, however, and heaven and earth are set infinitely apart. If you wish to see the truth then hold no opinions for or against anything. To set up what you like against what you dislike is the disease of the mind.
>
> —*Seng-ts'an*, Hsin-hsin Ming

INDEX

ABOUT THE AUTHORS

Since 1987, award-winning authors, seminar leaders, and business consultants Ariel and Shya Kane have acted as guides, leading people through the swamp of the mind into clarity and brilliance of the moment. The Kanes's transformational approach has a unique flavor that is designed for modern-day circumstances and complexities while resonating with the universal truths of the ages.

Contact the Kanes

To find out more about the Kanes or to sign up to receive Ariel and Shya's podcasts and newsletters, visit their website: www.TransformationMadeEasy.com.

Also from Ariel and Shya Kane

How to Create
a Magical Relationship

0-07-160110-4

$15.95